TH[...] D1104743

The Clouds stands as the most controversial of Aristophanes' plays. For in this slashing attack on sophism, Socrates, revered by later centuries as philosopher and martyr, is singled out and portrayed as a venial trickster, a ludicrous and lamentable purveyor of intellectual corruption.

Whatever the reasons for this character assassination, however, the play itself transcends all misgivings. Filled with parody, exaggeration, outrageous burlesque, masterfully juggling ideas and reputations, it triumphantly remains as a magnificent display of comic genius. As William Arrowsmith writes, "In this play, for the first time, we catch a glimpse of that exquisite tension between slapstick and poetry, the obscene and the sublime, which was Aristophanes' major contribution to comedy."

WILLIAM ARROWSMITH was born in New Jersey in 1924, and received degrees from Princeton and Oxford Universities. He has been a Rhodes Scholar, a Woodrow Wilson Fellow, a Guggenheim Fellow, and the recipient of the Prix de Rome as well as numerous other distinguished awards. Not only has Professor Arrowsmith won recognition as one of the foremost classical teachers, scholars, and translators in the English-speaking world, he also has been a prime mover and shaper of the dramatic resurgence of the art of translation witnessed in America in recent years.

Recommended MENTOR Books

THE CLOUDS

BY ARISTOPHANES

Translated by: WILLIAM ARROWSMITH

THE MENTOR GREEK COMEDY
General Editor: WILLIAM ARROWSMITH

A MENTOR BOOK from
NEW AMERICAN LIBRARY
TIMES MIRROR
New York and Scarborough, Ontario
The New English Library Limited, London

MENTOR TRADEMARK REG. U.S. PAT. OFF. AND FOREIGN COUNTRIES
REGISTERED TRADEMARK—MARCA REGISTRADA
HECHO EN CHICAGO, U.S.A.

SIGNET, SIGNET CLASSICS, MENTOR, PLUME, MERIDIAN AND NAL
BOOKS are published *in the United States* by
The New American Library, Inc.,
1633 Broadway, New York, New York 10019,
in Canada by The New American Library of Canada Limited,
81 Mack Avenue, Scarborough, Ontario M1L 1M8,
in the United Kingdom by The New English Library Limited,
Barnard's Inn, Holborn, London, EC1N 2JR, England.

  6 7 8 9 10 11 12 13 14

PRINTED IN THE UNITED STATES OF AMERICA

CONTENTS

For John K. Colby

who first taught me Greek

INTRODUCTION

The Play

The original version of *The Clouds* was presented in March, 423 B.C. at the Great Dionysia, where it disappointed Aristophanes' hopes by being placed third. The First Prize was awarded to the aging Kratinos for his final comedy, *Pytine* (or *The Wineflask*) and the runner-up was Ameipsias with his *Konnos*.[1] After the success of both *Acharnians* and *Knights*, this defeat must have been a bitter blow for Aristophanes. In *Knights* of the year before he had twitted Kratinos with being a doddering drunkard whose comic talents had decayed, and the drunkard had replied by confessing his drunkenness in a play of such comic verve and gaiety—accusing Aristophanes, for instance, of being a mere "Euripidaristophanizing" plagiarist—that he completely defeated his brash young critic. Worse yet, Ameipsias' *Konnos* was, like *The Clouds*, an attack on the sophistic movement, containing a Chorus of Sophists and, evidently, satirizing Sokrates by name. All this might not have mattered had *The Clouds* been a less ambitious play, but Aristophanes regarded it as by far the finest comedy of his career to date.[2]

Probably in the hope of getting a second hearing—if only from readers—he revised the play, and the version of *The Clouds* which we now possess is not the original of 423 B.C. but a revision carried out some three or four years later.

[1] Konnos was the name of Sokrates' music teacher, and it is likely that the play attacked the "New Music."
[2] *The Clouds*, 522: "convinced . . . that this play was the finest of my comedies . . ."

According to the Scholiast, the revision was thorough and
extensive changes were made, but the chief alterations affected
three sections in particular: the *parabasis*, the *agon* between
the two *Logoi*, and the finale, the burning of the Thinkery.
The full extent of these changes cannot be ascertained. In the
parabasis, the original choral anapests were replaced by a
passage whose meter is unique in a *parabasis* (a probable
indication that the poet had no expectation of seeing the play
restaged) and in which Aristophanes takes off the customary
choral mask and speaks to his readers directly in the first
person. To the *agon* was added the famous, passionate defense
of the Old Education, a speech clearly designed, through its
power of conviction and moral seriousness, to show Aristophanes' critics that what was at stake in this play was nothing
less than the fate and future of civilized Athens. About the
finale no such certainty is possible, though there is some small
reason to believe that in the original version it was the god
Hermes, rather than Strepsiades, who fired the Thinkery.

Even in its present form, revised for readers rather than for
the stage, *The Clouds* is visibly a masterpiece, a play of wonderful, ragging satire, tilted so expertly toward the preposterous
and the absurd that its effect is wholly and unmistakably comic.
We have, in fact, almost a *reductio ad absurdum* of the satiri-
cal intent, satire become so *buffa* and burlesque that its characters and targets, by sheer exaggeration and incongruity
survive as directly comic. In short, a splendid play, beautifully
sustained and shaped, and everywhere guided by Aristophanes'
genius for comic distortion and his cunning of absurdity. If not
the funniest play he ever wrote, it is certainly the cleverest:
clever in construction and plot, clever in its exploitation of
incongruities, clever in polemic and wit. Almost, perhaps, too
clever for its own good. But for Aristophanes these very qualities of cleverness and wit were precisely what made *The
Clouds* superior to his own previous work and that of his
"cheap and vulgar rivals": for their slapstick of situation and
crude horseplay he here substitutes the ludicrous slapstick of
the intellect and the better horseplay of poetry and imagination. In its structure too *The Clouds* is an improvement.
Unusually tight and coherent,[3] at least by Aristophanic stand-

---

[3] In my opinion the only major structural flaw in the play is the
abrupt change in the role of the Chorus. At least I find a jar when
the Clouds suddenly reveal that they are actually celestial *agents
provocateurs* masking as the patrons of the Sophists.

ards, its action is all of a piece, a continuously unfolding plot, written to be performed by a small cast, and singlemindedly devoted to the pursuit of its quarry. If it lacks the miraculous violence and vigor of *The Knights* or the exuberance of *The Acharnians*, it makes up for those qualities by the greater clarity and economy of its design and the pure lyricism of its poetry. Until *The Birds*, there is nothing in Aristophanes to match the loveliness of the poetry here assigned to the Chorus of Clouds as it enters. In this play, for the first time, we catch a glimpse of that exquisite tension between slapstick and poetry, the obscene and the sublime, which was Aristophanes' major individual contribution to comedy and which lies at the heart of his two greatest lyrical comedies, *The Birds* and *The Frogs*.

At first blush the improbable victim of *The Clouds* seems to be the philosopher Sokrates. But actually Aristophanes is deliberately exploiting Sokrates here as a convenient comic representative of the sophistic corruption which is the play's real subject. In the illustration of that corruption, Sokrates is nothing more than the poet's cipher, a curious catchpaw of those enormous cultural polarities (Old and New, Tradition and Innovation, Country and City, Peace and War, Poetry and Prose, Custom and Logic, etc.) which Aristophanes loved to elaborate and which he presented in play after play as locked in a life-and-death struggle for the soul of Athens. Whether Aristophanes privately believed that Sokrates was a Sophist or presented him that way for its comic and preposterous effect, we shall never know. But for the purposes of the play, Sokrates is merely a genial polemical emblem of the sophistic movement—if that extraordinary simultaneous flowering of individual genius, crankery, "educationism," and fraud can be called a movement at all. For Aristophanes such distinctions are academic, and to his mind the Sophists are a movement only because they are something worse, a conspiracy of charlatans and humbugs. Distinctions of doctrine and belief are totally disregarded. Jumbled together in ludicrous proximity and then stuffed into the mouth of Sokrates are the doctrines of Protagoras, the pre-Socratics generally, Anaxagoras, Diagoras, Gorgias, Prodikos, and perhaps Thrasymachos. It is grotesque —and hilarious. It is polemic on the grand scale, contemptuous of niceties, careless of reputations, unfair, Procrustean, and passionately loyal to its central perception. Addressed to, and exploiting, the average man's ridiculous stereotype of philosophy and science, it remains an honest and uncompromising play.

Grant Aristophanes his premises, and his logic is ruthlessly consistent. If Sokrates is a symbol of intellectual corruption and fraud, Strepsiades represents the Old Tradition in its corruption. Far from presenting Sokrates as the indispensable corrupter, Aristophanes shows that Strepsiades can be hoodwinked only because he had been corrupted *prior* to his enrollment in the Thinkery. All Sokrates does is to complete the process—or at least he tries to. But for Aristophanes the Sophists are merely symptoms of the general corruption, not its causes; they stand to education and the life of the mind exactly as Kleon stands to politics and Euripides to tragedy. If the Sophists are strong in being unprincipled, Strepsiades is weak because he is stupid and because the principles and values that might have protected him from his own stupidity have deteriorated. He is essentially only a denser Dikaiopolis become citified and decadent; in another context he might have been a peasant hero. But transplanted to Athens from the country, cursed with an expensive aristocratic marriage and a playboy son, he is an Awful Warning on the Perils of the City and the Evils of Imperialism. According to Aristophanes, the process of corruption began with Athenian imperialism and the war fought to maintain the empire. If imperialism brought with it tyranny, luxury, litigation, and the domination of political life by demagogic rhetoric, the war was destroying the very fabric of Athenian life by ravaging the countryside and forcing the evacuation of the country population into the city. There, cut off from the earth and uprooted from the context that gave it life and value, the Old Order had decayed, and with it were being destroyed all those traditions and virtues and decencies which, for a conservative countryman like Aristophanes, were synonymous with Athenian civilization itself. Strepsiades is his comic image of this corruption and Sokrates its aggravating symptom. If the causes were irremediable, he could at least struggle with the symptoms. And no quarter asked or given.

Aristophanes and Sokrates

Why did Aristophanes select Sokrates as his spokesman for the Sophists, and was he guilty of malicious slander and moral irresponsibility in so doing?

By now these two questions have become inextricably bound up with the fortunes of the play which is, ironically, more commonly read as a perverse adjunct to The Socratic Problem than for its satire of the Sophists. No definite answer is possible in the poor state of our evidence, but the questions cannot be shrugged off, and I offer the following considerations for what they may be worth.

1. Plato's charge against Aristophanes is the serious charge of moral irresponsibility. By circulating a distorted image of Sokrates, Aristophanes created, or abetted, those slanders which Plato believed led to Sokrates' death. The official indictment read: "Sokrates is a malefactor who meddles in the matters of the heavens and the earth below, who makes the Worse Argument appear the Better and teaches others to follow his example." And the Platonic Sokrates comments to the jury: "You yourselves have seen these very things in Aristophanes' comedy—a Sokrates who is carried around in a basket and asserts that he walks upon the air and a great many other absurdities, of which I am completely ignorant." We *may*, if we wish, doubt Plato's interpretation, but presumably the charges are accurately reported, and the implication is clear: the slanders of *The Clouds*, directly or indirectly, created the formal accusation brought against Sokrates in 399 B.C.

2. But the evidence is partisan and polemical. Plato's account is that of a devoted disciple, not a reporter, and the prejudice of Platonists is almost religious.[4]

3. Sokrates' own reaction, if Plutarch can be trusted,[5] was not that he had been slandered but that he had been teased: "I am twitted in the theater as I would be at a drinking-party."

4. Nonetheless, judging from the available evidence, the

[4] It has even been suggested that *The Clouds* failed to win First Prize because the audience recognized—and disliked—the distorted image of Sokrates. Given what happened to Sokrates, this seems excessively naive.

[5] *De educatione puerorum* xiv.

caricature of Sokrates in *The Clouds* is so distorted that it cannot be called a caricature at all. Thus Sokrates refused payment, was not an atheist, had no Thinkery, and never held the doctrines which are here put into his mouth. Worse, he consistently attacked the Sophists and their doctrines. He does, however, admit in the *Apology* that in his earlier days he had dabbled in "scientific" research.

5. That Aristophanes could not have foretold the consequence of his "slanders" is irrelevant. Slander is slander.

6. Aristophanes' private opinion of Sokrates is also irrelevant. In Plato's *Symposium,* the two men are presented as being on friendly terms, but this does not entitle us to suppose that Aristophanes really admired Sokrates or thought his views anything but pernicious. If it does, then Aristophanes was a hypocrite as well as morally irresponsible.

7. If Aristophanes was really ignorant of Sokrates' beliefs, he is equally culpable. Ignorance is no excuse for slander. But Aristophanes was anything but an ignorant man, and his refusal to allow his Sokrates to make one statement that is recognizably Sokratic seems to me to indicate strategy rather than stupidity.

8. The distortions practiced upon Sokrates are typical and not exceptional. They are, for instance, completely of a piece with Aristophanes' systematic distortion of Euripides; if Euripides' words are quoted against him, they are invariably taken from their context and parodied by willful misunderstanding. But those who are angered by the spectacle of Sokrates mocked have never lifted a finger in defense of Euripides.[6]

9. In any case, the treatment of Sokrates is *not*, by Aristophanic standards, harsh or "pitiless satire," as Platonists claim. It is, in fact, surprisingly mild and impersonal. (The savage attack upon Kleon in *The Knights* is an instructive comparison.) Thus, apart from a couple of gibes at Sokrates' gait and general bathlessness, his personal life is strictly avoided. We hear nothing of the shrewish Xanthippe, nothing of the fashionable pederasty of the Socratic circle (or at least nothing that implicates Sokrates), nothing about Sokrates' midwife-mother (*cf.* the treatment meted out to Euripides' mother), etc. The charges are wholly professional: Sokrates is a humbug and a charlatan.

10. Aristophanes' "slanders" are, in some real sense, dic-

---

[6] As Speaker of the House Rayburn said in a different context: "It all depends on *whose* ox is gettin' gored."

tated by convention. Comedy is the heir of the early *komos*, and the *komos* was a convention whose essential attributes were invective and abuse. Which is to say merely that the Athenian comedian was not merely given license to be abusive, but that abuse was *expected* of him. And precisely because it was conventional, was expected, it could be discounted as conventional; and presumably those who were ragged were expected to take their ragging in good part—as Sokrates did, though Kleon (and Plato) did not. Needless to say, such a convention makes the notion of "moral irresponsibility" extremely hard to assess.

11. Sokrates is presented as preposterous and this strikes me as cool and deliberate strategy—doubtless sustained by malice and even a little contempt. There is, after all, a kind of humor—the kind of humor of the *komos*, I suspect—which contrives its fun out of a total inversion of the truth. Because the humor is conventional, the exaggeration is understood *as* exaggeration and the humorist's success consists in the very size and absurdity of the distortion. The comedy lies in the disparity between the known truth and the degree of distortion achieved. This explanation might be less acceptable if it were not for the fact that Aristophanes is, of all comedians, the master of the incongruous, and that the stunning distortion is everywhere his stock-in-trade.

12. If Aristophanes has not made Sokrates preposterous because the preposterousness was funny, he has done so out of dislike and the conviction that Sokrates was dangerous. In this he was probably mistaken, but Aristophanes was a man in the livery of an Idea, and if Sokrates is distorted or satirized in the service of that Idea, it is regrettable but not culpable. Ideas distort the world and those who serve them. Platonists should understand.

Text and Acknowledgments

The texts which I have used as a basis of this translation are primarily those of Cantarella and Coulon, and I am, like every other translator of Aristophanes, indebted to B. B. Rogers' splendid notes and commentaries on individual passages. To both the University of California at Riverside and the University of Texas I owe my thanks for generous grants for the preparation of the manuscript. For help and encouragement and criticism, I am indebted to a great many people, but particularly to Douglass Parker and to my wife.

WILLIAM ARROWSMITH

Characters of the Play

STREPSIADES, *father of Pheidippides*

PHEIDIPPIDES, *a playboy*

XANTHIAS, *a slave*

STUDENTS OF SOKRATES

SOKRATES

CHORUS OF CLOUDS

KORYPHAIOS, *or Chorus Leader*

ARISTOPHANES

PHILOSOPHY

SOPHISTRY

PASIAS, *creditor of Strepsiades*

AMYNIAS, *creditor of Strepsiades*

CHAIREPHON, *disciple of Sokrates*

SLAVES, STUDENTS, WITNESSES, etc.

SCENE: *A street in Athens. On the left, the house of Strepsiades,* an old farmer compelled by the war to leave the country and take up residence in Athens; on the right, the tiny, grubby, ramshackle hovel which houses Sokrates' Thinkery. On the extreme left, a statue of Poseidon. Before Strepsiades' house stands a Herm, a bust of the god Hermes supported by a square pillar; in front of Sokrates' house, balancing the Herm, stands a pot-bellied stove with a long tapering flue and a placard which reads:* MODEL OF THE UNIVERSE ACCORDING TO THE CONVECTION PRINCIPLE.

Two cots are placed before Strepsiades' house, one occupied by Strepsiades himself, the other by Pheidippides. Huddled on the ground nearby lie several loudly snoring slaves. The time is just before dawn.

STREPSIADES

Thrashing restlessly, then throwing off his blankets and sitting bolt upright. He yawns.

Yaaaahhuuuuu.
Great Zeus Almighty, what an endless monster
of a night it's been! Won't the daylight *ever* come?
I could have sworn I heard the roosters crowing hours
ago.
    And listen to those slaves. Still snoring away!
By god, things around here were a long sight different
in the good old days before this war! Drat
this stinking war anyway! It's ruined Athens.
Why, you can't even whip your own slaves any more
or they'll desert to the Spartans.*
                                    Bah.

Pointing to Pheidippides.

And as for *him*,
that precious playboy son of mine, he's worse yet.
Look at him, stretched out there sleeping like a log
under five fat blankets, farting away.

—All right,
if that's the way you want it, boy, I'll snuggle down
and fart you back a burst or two.

*He burrows under the blankets for a moment, then
throws them off and sits up again.*

DAMN!
I'm so bitten up by all these blasted bedbuggering debts
and bills and stables-fees, I can't catch a wink.

Turning on Pheidippides.

And all because of YOU!
Yes, you and your damned horses!
Gigs, rigs, nags, ponytails*. . . . Hell,
horses everywhere! Horses in your dreams!

But *me?*
I'm bankrupt, broke, ruined, waiting for the end of the
month when all these debts come due.

Savagely kicking Xanthias awake.

—You. You there,
light me a lamp and bring me my ledger.

*The slave rises, lights a flickering lamp, and brings
him the ledger.*

Now then,
I'll just run over this account of my debts and see
how much I owe.
Hmmmm.

Reading aloud.

TO PASIAS: *THE SUM OF
THREE HUNDRED—*
Three hundred to Pasias? What in god's name for?
Of course. I remember. That gelding I bought him. Idiot!
Better I should have gelded myself.

PHEIDIPPIDES

Shouting in his sleep.

PHILO,
YOU FOULED ME! KEEP IN YOUR OWN
LANE!

STREPSIADES

That's it.
That's the horsey blight that has blasted me dead.
Even in his dreams he thinks he's winning the derby.

PHEIDIPPIDES

In his sleep.

HOW MANY LAPS FOR THE STEEPLE-
CHASE?

STREPSIADES

Laps, is it?
A fat lot of laps you've driven your poor old man!

Resuming his accounting.

Let's see now. What's the next entry after Pasias?

Reading aloud.

TO AMYNIAS: FOR GIG, BODY AND WHEELS
INCLUDED, THE SUM OF—

PHEIDIPPIDES

In his sleep.

ROLL THE HORSE IN
THE DUST, TRAINER, AND THEN STABLE HIM.

STREPSIADES

You've rolled *me* out of house and
home, damn you!
I've lost two or three lawsuits on your account and now
the other creditors are clamoring for confiscation.

PHEIDIPPIDES

Waking up crossly.

Damn it,
Dad, why do you have to thrash around like this all night
long?

STREPSIADES

Because there's a bumbailiff* in the mattress biting me,
that's why.

PHEIDIPPIDES

Oh, for god's sake, let me sleep, will you?

STREPSIADES

Go on, damn you, sleep! But I give you warning, boy.
Someday these debts will land on *your* head.

Pheidippides' only answer is a snore.

By god,
I hope that meddling matchmaker who prodded me on
to marry your mother dies a nasty death!
I used to be a farmer—the sweetest life on earth,
a lovely, moldy, unspruce, litter-jumbled life,
bursting with honeybees, bloated with sheep and olives.
And then, poor hick, what did I do but marry
your mother, a city girl, and niece of that Megakles
who was son and heir of old Blueblood Megakles* himself?
She was a pretty piece: Miss Megakles-de-luxe.
Well, so we go married and we clambered into bed—
me, a stink of wine-lees, fig-boxes, and wool-fat;
she, the whiff of spices, pure saffron, tonguekisses,
Luxury, High Prices, gourmandizing, goddess Lechery,
and every little elf, imp, and sprite of Intercourse.
But I'll say this for your mother: she was a worker.
Nothing slow about *her*. All day long she'd sit there
working away at her loom and shoving in the wool,
and then in bed at night she'd work on me
for more.
Expense meant nothing.
Clipped?
I was *shorn*.

"Madam," I said, "what do you think I am? A man
or a goat?"

Suddenly the oil lamp sputters and goes out.

XANTHIAS

There's no oil left in the lamp.

STREPSIADES

Jackass!

And why in god's name did you light that guzzler of a lamp?
Come here and be whipped.

XANTHIAS

But why? What have *I* done?

STREPSIADES

Because you put in potbellied wicks, that's why.

*He lunges at Xanthias who ducks away and dis-
appears into the house.*

Anyway, when that darling brat of ours was born
to the missues and me, we immediately started squabbling
over his name. She, of course, wanted something fancy,
some upperclass, high-horse handle with *hippos** in it—
Xanth*ippos* or Char*ippos* or Kall*ippi*des—while I naturally
wanted to give him the fine old name of Pheidonides*
in honor of his thrifty grandfather. Well, we haggled
and at last agreed on a compromise name: Pheidippides.*
She used to gush over the baby: "Just imagine. Some day
he'll be an important man, just like his Uncle Megakles,
and drive in his purple robes up to the Akropolis."
And I'd put in: "Ha, drive his goats from the hills,
you mean, dressed like his dad in a filthy smock."
Well, needless to say, he paid no heed to me
and now he's ended up by squirting his dirty horse-pox
all over my money.
                                Anyway, after beating my brains
all night long, I think I've finally found a way,
the *only* way out, a wonderful little chink of a loophole.
Now if I can only shove him through it, I'm saved.

But first I've got to find some way of waking him up.
I wonder what's the nicest way to wake up.

Hmmmm.

Cooing in Pheidippides' ear.

Pheidippides.
Little Pheidippides.

PHEIDIPPIDES

Waking angrily.

Damn it, Dad, what *now?*

STREPSIADES

Give your Old Man a kiss. There, now your hand, son.

PHEIDIPPIDES

Look here, what's this all about?

STREPSIADES

Tell me, my boy,
are you *really* fond of your poor old father?

PHEIDIPPIDES

Sure, Dad.

I swear it. So help me Poseidon.

STREPSIADES

No, NOT THAT!
For god's sake, none of those horse-god oaths* of yours!
Poseidon indeed! That god's the cause of all my troubles.
But if you *really* love me, my boy, I beg you, implore you,
do what I ask.

Please.

PHEIDIPPIDES

Suspiciously.

Depends. What are you asking?

STREPSIADES

Reform yourself, boy. Change your whole way of life.
Follow my advice and make a new man of yourself.
A fresh Pheidippides.

PHEIDIPPIDES

But how?

STREPSIADES

First promise.

PHEIDIPPIDES

Reluctantly.

I promise.
So help me—Dionysos.

STREPSIADES

Good. Now then, look over there.
Do you see that dirty little hovel with the dinky door?

PHEIDIPPIDES

Yes. But what are you driving at, Dad?

STREPSIADES

Awesomely.

My boy,
that little hovel is the Thinkery. Intellectuals live there,
professors who will teach you—and what's more, *prove* it—
that the whole atmosphere is actually a Cosmical Oven*
and we're not really people but little bits of charcoal
blazing away. What's more—for a fee,* of course—
they offer a course called *The Technique of Winning
Lawsuits.** Honest or dishonest, it's all one.

PHEIDIPPIDES

Who are they?

STREPSIADES

Great Scholars. Scientists.

PHEIDIPPIDES

Fine. Who are they?

STREPSIADES

Er . . .

Gentlemen. Men of Learning.

PHEIDIPPIDES

Yes, but what are their *names?*

STREPSIADES

Why . . .

PHEIDIPPIDES

Oh lord, I know those filthy charlatans you mean—
those frauds, those barefoot pedants with the look of death,
Chairephon and that humbug, Sokrates.

STREPSIADES

Scandalized.

Here, here, boy.
Hush. For shame. Don't ever let me hear you talking
so disrespectfully. What's more, if you don't want
your poor Old Man to starve, you'd better go study there
and ditch your damn horses.

PHEIDIPPIDES

By Dionysos, I *won't!*
Not on your life. I wouldn't go there if you bribed me
with every racehorse in Leogoras' stable!

STREPSIADES

My dearest boy,
I implore you. *Please* go and study at the Thinkery.

PHEIDIPPIDES

Study *what?*

STREPSIADES

        I've heard that they teach two kinds of Logic.*
One of them is called Philosophical, or Moral, Logic—
whatever *that* may be. The other one is called
Sophistic, or Sokratic, Logic. Now, if you could learn
this second Logic, I wouldn't have to pay a penny
of all those debts you've saddled me with.

PHEIDIPPIDES

                    Count me out.
I'd rather die. Why, those vampires would suck me dry.
They'd scrape the tan right off my face. How could I
face the fellows down at the track?

STREPSIADES

           Then, by Demeter,
you've had your last meal on me. Take your critturs
and pack out of this house and be damned to you!

PHEIDIPPIDES

                  Uncle Megakles
won't let me go horseless for long. I'll go to him.
The hell with you.

Exit Pheidippides.

STREPSIADES

        I'm down, but not for long.
First I'll say a little prayer to the gods, and then
I'll go and enroll at the Thinkery myself.
                But whoa:
at my age the memory is bad, the intellect dull.
How could I ever master that hair-splitting logic?
Still, I have to go, so why am I dawdling here
instead of banging on the door?

*He walks over to Sokrates' house and kicks
at the door.*

                —Hey, porter!

STUDENT

From within.

  Go bang yourself.

Opening the door.

                    Who are you to kick our door?

STREPSIADES

Strepsiades, son of Pheidon. From Kikynna.

STUDENT

By god, the way you come here and kick in our door
I think your name should damn well be Stupidities.
Do you realize that you've just caused the miscarriage*
of a great scientific discovery?

STREPSIADES

Humbly apologetic.

                         Oh, please excuse me.
I didn't realize. You see, I come from the country.
But tell me, what discovery miscarried?

STUDENT

                              It's top secret.
Classified information. Access only to students.

STREPSIADES

You can tell *me* then. That's why I've come here,
to be a student at the Thinkery.

STUDENT

                         In that case, very well.
But remember, our researches are solemn mysteries.

Whispering.

                                   Listen.
Just a minute ago Sokrates was questioning Chairephon
about the number of fleafeet a flea could broadjump.

You see, a flea happened to bite Chairephon on the eyebrow
and then vaulted across and landed on Sokrates' head.

STREPSIADES

How did he measure it?

STUDENT

A stroke of absolute genius.
First he melted some wax. Then he caught the flea,
dipped its tiny feet in the melted wax,
let it cool, and lo! little Persian bootees.
He slipped the bootees off and measured the distance.

STREPSIADES

Lord Zeus, what exquisite finesse of mind!

STUDENT

Elementary really. You haven't heard *anything* yet.
Would you like another sample?

STREPSIADES

Oh, I'd *like* that. Go on.

STUDENT

Well, it seems that Chairephon was asking Sokrates
which of two theories he held: that gnats tootled
through their mouths or, in reverse, through their tails.

STREPSIADES

Eagerly.

Gosh. Go on. What was his theory about the gnat?

STUDENT

Attend.

According to him, the intestinal tract of the gnat
is of puny proportions, and through this diminutive duct
the gastric gas of the gnat is forced under pressure
down to the rump. At that point the compressed gases,

as through a narrow valve, escape with a whoosh,
thereby causing the characteristic tootle or cry
of the flatulent gnat.

STREPSIADES

So the gnat has a bugle up its ass!
O thrice-blessèd mortals! What bowel-wisdom!
Why, the man who has mastered the ass of the gnat
could win an acquittal from any court!

STUDENT

And you know,
just the other day he was cheated of an immense discovery
because of a lizard.

STREPSIADES

Cheated by a *lizard?* But how?

STUDENT

It happened at night, during the course of his researches on
the orbit of the moon. There he stood, gaping wide-mouthed
at the sky, when a lizard on the roof let loose on him.

STREPSIADES

Ha! A lizard crapping on Sokrates! That's rich.

STUDENT

And last night there was nothing in school to eat.

STREPSIADES

Goodness,
how did he ever manage your supper?

STUDENT

A combination
of science and legerdemain.
He quickly sprinkled the table
with a fine film of powderlike ashes. Then,
deftly bending a skewer in the shape of a compass

he drew a vast arc along whose perimeter
the hook of his compass encountered somebody's cloak.
Quickly flicking his hand, he pulled back compass
and catch. He pawned the cloak; we ate the proceeds.

STREPSIADES

Why, Thales himself was an amateur compared to this!
Throw open the Thinkery! Unbolt the door
and let me see this wizard Sokrates in person.
Open up! I'm MAD for education!

*The ekkyklema is wheeled about to show the whole
interior court of Sokrates' Thinkery. High overhead
the crane supports Sokrates in his basket busily
scanning the heavens. Hanging on the walls of the
Thinkery are various charts, maps, instruments, etc.
In the center of the courtyard stand a number of
utterly pale, emaciated students deeply engaged in
a rapt contemplation of the ground.*

Great Herakles,
what kind of zoo is this?

STUDENT

What's so strange about it?
What do you take them for?

STREPSIADES

Spartan prisoners
from Pylos.* But why are they all staring at the ground?

STUDENT

They're engaged in geological research:* a survey
of the earth's strata.

STREPSIADES

Of course. Looking for truffles.

To one of the students.

—You there, don't strain yourself looking. I know
where they grow big and beautiful.

Pointing to other students who are bent completely double.

> Hey, and look there:
what are those fellows doing bent over like that?

STUDENT

Those are graduate students doing research on Hades.

STREPSIADES

On Hades? Then why are their asses scanning the skies?

STUDENT

Taking a minor in Astronomy.

To the students.

> —Quick, inside with you.
Hurry, before the Master catches you.

STREPSIADES

> No, wait.
Let them stay a little longer. I want to speak to them
on a *private* matter.

STUDENT

> Impossible. The statutes clearly forbid
overexposure to fresh air.

*The students disappear through a door at the rear.
Strepsiades meanwhile is staring at the various maps
and instruments on the walls.*

STREPSIADES

Pointing to a chart.

> In the name of heaven,
what's *that?*

STUDENT

> That's for astronomy.

STREPSIADES

Pointing to surveying instruments.

And what are those?

STUDENT

They're for geometry.

STREPSIADES

Geometry? And what's that good for?

STUDENT

Surveying, of course.

STREPSIADES

Surveying what? Lots?

STUDENT

No. The whole world.

STREPSIADES

What a clever gadget!
And as patriotic as it is useful.*

STUDENT

Pointing to a map.

Now then, over here
we have a map of the entire world. You see there?
That's Athens.

STREPSIADES

That, Athens? Don't be ridiculous.
Why, I can't see even a single lawcourt in session.*

STUDENT

Nonetheless, it's quite true. It really is Athens.

STREPSIADES

Then where are my neighbors of Kikynna?

STUDENT

Here they are.
And you see this island squeezed along the coast?
That's Euboia.

STREPSIADES

I know that place well enough.
Perikles squeezed it dry.* But where's Sparta?

STUDENT

Sparta? Right over here.

STREPSIADES

That's MUCH TO CLOSE!
You'd be well advised to move it further away.

STUDENT

But that's utterly impossible.

STREPSIADES

You'll be sorry you didn't,
by god.

*For the first time Strepsiades catches sight of
Sokrates in his basket overhead.*

Look: who's that dangling up there in the basket?

STUDENT

Himself.

STREPSIADES

Who's Himself?

STUDENT

Sokrates.

STREPSIADES

SOKRATES!
Then call him down. Go on. Give a great big shout.

STUDENT

Hastily and apprehensively taking his leave.

Er . . . *you* call him. I'm a busy man.

Exit Student.

STREPSIADES

O Sokrates!

No answer from the basket.

Yoohoo. Sokrates!

SOKRATES

From a vast philosophical height.

Well, creature of a day?

STREPSIADES

What in the world are you doing up there?

SOKRATES

Ah, sir,
I walk upon the air and look down upon the sun
from a superior standpoint.

STREPSIADES

Well, I suppose it's better
that you sneer at the gods from a basket up in the air
than do it down here on the ground.

SOKRATES

Precisely. You see,
only by being suspended aloft, by dangling
my mind in the heavens and mingling my rare thought
with the ethereal air, could I ever achieve strict
scientific accuracy in my survey of the vast empyrean.
Had I pursued my inquiries from down there on the ground,
my data would be worthless. The earth, you see, pulls down
the delicate essence of thought to its own gross level.

As an afterthought.

Much the same thing happens with watercress.

STREPSIADES

Ecstatically bewildered.

You don't say?
Thought draws down . . . delicate essence . . . into
watercress. O dear little Sokrates, please come down.
Lower away, and teach me what I need to know!

Sokrates is slowly lowered earthwards.

SOKRATES

What subject?

STREPSIADES

Your course on public speaking and debating techniques.
You see, my creditors have become absolutely ferocious.
You should see how they're hounding me. What's more,
Sokrates, they're about to seize my belongings.

SOKRATES

How in the
world could you fall so deeply in debt without realizing it?

STREPSIADES

How? A great, greedy horse-pox ate me up, that's how.
But that's why I want instruction in your second Logic,
you know the one—the get-away-without-paying argument.
I'll pay you *any* price you ask. I swear it.
By the gods.

SOKRATES

By the gods? The gods, my dear simple fellow,
are a mere expression coined by vulgar superstition.
We frown upon such coinage here.

STREPSIADES

What do *you* swear by?
Bars of iron, like the Byzantines?*

SOKRATES

Tell me, old man,
would you honestly like to learn the truth, the *real* truth,
about the gods?

STREPSIADES

By Zeus, I sure would. The *real* truth.

SOKRATES

And also be admitted to intercourse with their Serene
Highnesses, our goddesses, the Clouds?

STREPSIADES

Intercourse with *real*
goddesses? Oh yes, I'd *like* that.

SOKRATES

Very well. First, however,
you must take your seat upon the mystical couch.*

STREPSIADES

I'm sitting.

SOKRATES

And now we place this sacrificial wreath on your head.

STREPSIADES

A *sacrificial* wreath?
Hey, NO!
Please, Sokrates,
don't murder me like poor Athamas* in Sophokles' play!

SOKRATES

Athamas was saved. You must mean Phrixos.

STREPSIADES

                              Athamas,
Phrixos—so who's a critic? Dead is dead.

SOKRATES

Courage, gaffer. This is normal procedure, required
of all our initiates alike.

STREPSIADES

                    Yeah? What's in it for me?

SOKRATES

*Sprinkling Strepsiades from head to toe with ritual
flour.*

You shall be reborn, sir, as the perfect flower of orators,
a consummate, blathering, tinkling rascal.

STREPSIADES

                              That's no joke.
I'll be all flour the way you're powdering me.

SOKRATES

Silence!
        Holy hush command your tongue. Listen to my
prayer.

He stretches out his hands to heaven and prays.

*O Lord God Immeasurable Ether, You who envelop the
   world! O Translucent Ozone!*
                         And you, O lightningthundered
   holy Clouds!
Great Majesties, arise!
                   Reveal yourselves to your Sophist's
   eyes.

STREPSIADES

Whoa, ladies, don't rain yet. Don't get me wet. Let me wrap
up.

He wraps his head in his tunic.

What a damned fool! Coming without a hat.

SOKRATES

                                        Come forth,
be manifest, majestic Clouds! Reveal your forms to me.
And whether on Olympos' snow your brooding eyrie lies,
or on the waves you weave the dance with Ocean's lovely
     daughters,
or dip your golden pitchers in the waters of the Nile,
or hover on Mount Mimas' snows, or over Lake Maiotis—
come forth, great Clouds!
                         Accept our prayers!
                                             O hear us!
Amen.

From far off in the distance the Clouds are heard
singing. As they slowly approach Athens, the singing
increases steadily in volume as it rises in pitch.

CHORUS

                    Rise and soar
                    eternal Clouds!
                    Lift your loveliness of rain,
                    in sodden splendor come!
                    Soar from ocean's sullen swell,
                    rise higher to the peaks,
                    to the tall cliffs and trees!
                    Rise and soar,
                    while far below,
                    earth and shining harvest lie,
                    sound of god in river water,
                    blessèd ocean at its roar.
                    Arise!
                    For Ether's sleepless eye
                    now breaks with blazoned light!
                    Shake loose the rain,
                    immortal forms,
                    and walk upon the world!

A sustained burst of thunder is heard.

SOKRATES

O Clouds consummately blest, how clearly thy answer
rumbles!

To Strepsiades.

—Did you hear that thunder crack, that *basso profundo*
peal?

STREPSIADES

    And how!
All hail your holyships! What a nasty jolt you gave me!
What a ratatat! You scared me so I've got to thunder too.

He breaks wind.

Sacrilege on not, I'VE GOT TO CRAP!

SOKRATES

                      Silence, boor!
No more of your smut. Leave filth like that to the comic
stage.

A short low growl of thunder is heard.

Shhh.
    Quiet.
        The goddess swarm is stirring to its song.

CHORUS

          Virgins of rain,
          look on Pallas' shining earth,
          this oil-anointed land,
          country of Kekrops'
          hero-breeding plain!
          Holiness is here,
          home of the mysteries,
          whose unrevealable rites
          sanctify the soul.
          And here the gods have gifts.
          Below the splendid gables go
          processions of the blest,

and every season sees
its festivals, its crowns.
And early every Spring
Dionysos brings his joy,
the weaving of the dance,
the Muses and the flutes.

STREPSIADES

Holy Zeus, Sokrates, who were those ladies that sang
that solemn hymn? Were they heroines of mythology?

SOKRATES

No, old man.
Those were the Clouds of heaven, goddesses of men of
leisure and philosophers. To them we owe our repertoire of
verbal talents: our eloquence, intellect, fustian, casuistry,
force, wit, prodigious vocabulary, circumlocutory skill—

STREPSIADES

Suddenly carried away in cloudy inspiration.

Then that's why
I suddenly tingled all over—as though I were carried up,
buoyant, exalted, swollen somehow with the flatus of
philosophy: a mist of verbal fluff, a sudden unsubstantial
swelling, a tumid bubble of wrangling words, a windbag of
debate! I seemed rent by lightning speech, ah, the thrust
and parry of opinion, of minds massively meeting . . .
In short, Sokrates,
if I could see those ladies in person, I'd LOVE to.

SOKRATES

Then look over toward Parnes. I can see them settling down
ever so gently.

STREPSIADES

Where?

SOKRATES

There, a vast drifting swarm
nuzzling along through woods and valleys.

STREPSIADES

Rubbing his eyes.

I wonder what's wrong.

I can't see them.

SOKRATES

Look: just offstage.

STREPSIADES

Now I see them!

SOKRATES

You've got cataracts, friend, if you can't see them now.

*Slowly and majestically, the Chorus of Clouds files
in and takes up its position in the orchestra.*

STREPSIADES

Ooh, what venerable ladies! They take up all the space.

SOKRATES

And you actually mean to say that it's never occurred to you
that the Clouds of heaven were goddesses?

STREPSIADES

By Zeus, it's news to me.
I always used to think they were just fog and drizzle and
mist.

SOKRATES

Clearly then you must also be ignorant of the fact that the
Clouds are also patrons of a varied group of gentlemen,
comprising: chiropractors, prophets, longhairs, quacks, fops,
charlatans, fairies, dithyrambic poets, scientists, dandies,
astrologers, and other men of leisure. And because all
alike, without exception, walk with their heads among the
clouds and base their inspiration on the murky Muse, the
Clouds support them and feed them.

STREPSIADES

                        I see.
That's why they write*—
                     O downblow, dazed, of the sodden skies!
and
    *Ho, tresses of the Typho-headed gale! Ho, puffcheek
    squalls!*
or
   Spongy humus of the hyaline!
                        and
                        Hail, ye heaven-scudders,
sudden ospreys of the winds!
                     and
                   Come, ye wheeling cumuli,
ye clammy condensations, come!
                    And in return, these poets
gorge themselves on the flesh of the mullet and eat of the
breast of the thrush?

SOKRATES

And why not?

STREPSIADES

              But what I want to know is this:
why, if these ladies are really Clouds, they look like women?
For honest clouds aren't women.

SOKRATES

                    Then what *do* they look like?

STREPSIADES

I don't know for sure. Well, they look like mashed-up fluff,
not at all like women. No, by Zeus. Women have . . . noses.

SOKRATES

Would you mind if I asked you a question or two?

STREPSIADES

                     Go right ahead.

SOKRATES

Haven't you sometimes seen a cloud that looked like a
centaur? Or a leopard perhaps? Or a wolf? Or a bull?

STREPSIADES

Often. So what?

SOKRATES

Well, the Clouds assume whatever shape they wish. Now
suppose they happened to meet some shaggy, hairy beast of
a man—Hieronymos, for instance; instantly they turn into
wild centaurs as a caricature of his lust.

STREPSIADES

I see. But what if they
run into Simon, that swindler of government funds?

SOKRATES

Presto, they turn into wolves
and catch his likeness to a T.

STREPSIADES

Oh, I see. And yesterday
because they met that coward Kleonymos, they turned into
deer?

SOKRATES

Precisely. And just now, when they saw Kleisthenes in the
audience, they suddenly turned into women.

STREPSIADES

Welcome then, august Ladies!
Welcome, queens of heaven!
If ever you spoke to mortal man,
I implore you, speak to me!

A great burst of thunder.
Strepsiades cowers with fright.

KORYPHAIOS

Hail, superannuated man!
Hail, old birddog of culture!

To Sokrates.

And hail to you, O Sokrates,
high priest of poppycock!
Inform us what your wishes are.
For of all the polymaths on earth, it's you we most prefer—
you and Prodikos. Him we love for wisdom's sake, but you,
sir, for your swivel-eyes, your barefoot swagger down the
street, because you're poor on our account and terribly
affected.

STREPSIADES

Name of Earth, what a voice! Solemn and holy and awful!

SOKRATES

These are the only gods there are. The rest are but figments.

STREPSIADES

Holy name of Earth! Olympian Zeus is a figment?

SOKRATES

Zeus?
What Zeus?
Nonsense.
There is no Zeus.

STREPSIADES

No Zeus?
Then *who* makes it rain? Answer me that.

SOKRATES

Why, the Clouds,
of course.
What's more, the proof is incontrovertible.
For instance,
have you ever yet seen rain when you didn't see a cloud?

But if your hypothesis were correct, Zeus could drizzle
   from an empty sky
while the clouds were on vacation.

STREPSIADES

                    By Apollo, you're right. A pretty
   proof.
And to think I always used to believe the rain was just Zeus
pissing through a sieve.
                    All right, *who* makes it thunder?
Brrr. I get goosebumps just saying it.

SOKRATES

                    The Clouds again,
of course. A simple process of Convection.

STREPSIADES

                    I admire you,
but I don't follow you.

SOKRATES

          Listen. The Clouds are a saturate water-solution.
Tumescence in motion, of necessity, produces precipitation.
When these distended masses collide—*boom!*
                    Fulmination.

STREPSIADES

But who makes them move before they collide? Isn't that
Zeus?

SOKRATES

Not Zeus, idiot. The Convection-principle!

STREPSIADES

                    Convection? That's a
   new one.
Just think. So Zeus is out and convection-principle's in.
Tch, tch.
          But wait: you haven't told me who makes it thunder.

SOKRATES

But I just *finished* telling you! The Clouds are water-packed; they collide with each other and explode because of the pressure.

STREPSIADES

Yeah?
And what's your proof for *that*?

SOKRATES

Why, take yourself as example.
You know that meat-stew the vendors sell at the Panathenaia? How it gives you the cramps and your stomach starts to rumble?

STREPSIADES

Yes,
by Apollo! I remember. What an awful feeling! You feel sick and your belly churns and the fart rips loose like thunder. First just a gurgle, *pappapax;* then louder, *pappaPAPAXapaX,* and finally like thunder, *PAPAPAPAXAPAXAPPAPAXapap!*

SOKRATES

Precisely.
First think of the tiny fart that your intestines make.
Then consider the heavens: their infinite farting is thunder.
For thunder and farting are, in principle, one and the same.

STREPSIADES

Then where does lightning come from? And when it strikes why is it that some men are killed and others aren't even touched? Clearly it's *got* to be Zeus. He's behind it, blasting the liars with bolts of lightning.

SOKRATES

Look, you idiotic Stone-Age relic,
if Zeus strikes the liars with lightning, then why on earth is a man like Simon still alive? Or Kleonymos? Or Theoros?

They're liars ten times over.

                                   But no. Instead of doing that,
he shatters his own shrines, blasts the holiest place names
in Homer and splinters the great oaks. And why, I ask you?
Have you ever heard of an oak tree committing perjury?

STREPSIADES

                                                        Say,
you know, you've got something there. But how do you
explain the lightning?

SOKRATES

                         Attend.

Illustrating his lecture by means of the potbellied-
stove Model of the Universe.

                         Let us hypothesize a current of
   arid air
ascending heavenwards. Now then, as this funnelled flatus
slowly invades the limp and dropsical sacks of the Clouds,
they, in turn, begin to belly and swell, distended with gas
like a child's balloon when inflated with air. Then, so prodigious
become the pressures within that the cloud-casings burst
   apart,
exploding with that celestial ratatat called thunder and
   thereby releasing
the winds. These, in turn, whizz out at such incalculable
   velocities
that they catch on fire.
                         Result: lightning.

STREPSIADES

                                   The very same thing
   that happened to me
at the great feast of Zeus!
                         I was roasting myself a sausage
and forgot to slit the skin. Well, suddenly it bloated up
and SPLAT!
                  —singed my eyebrows off and splattered my
   face with guts.

CHORUS

—Ah, how he hungers after learning!

To Strepsiades.

      —Sir, if you can pass our test,
we guarantee that you shall be
      —the cynosure of Hellas.
—Our requirements are these:
      —First, is your memory keen?
—Do you hanker for researching?
      —Are you subject to fatigue
from standing up or walking?
      —Does winter weather daunt you?
—Can you go without a meal?
      —Abstain from wine and exercise?
—And keep away from girls?
      —Last, do you solemnly swear
adherence to our code?
    —*To wrangle*
      —*niggle*
       —*haggle*
        —*battle*
—*a loyal soldier of the Tongue, conducting yourself always
like a true philosopher.*

STREPSIADES

      Ladies, if all you require
is hard work, insomnia, worry, endurance, and a stomach
that eats anything, why, have no fear. For I'm your man
and as hard as nails.

SOKRATES

     And you promise to follow faithfully in
my path,
acknowledging no other gods but mine, to wit, the Trinity—
GREAT CHAOS, THE CLOUDS, and BAMBOOZLE?

STREPSIADES

        If I met
another god,
I'd cut him dead, so help me. Here and now I swear off
sacrifice and prayer forever.

KORYPHAIOS

Then, Sir, inform us boldly
what you wish. Providing you honor and revere the Clouds
and faithfully pursue the Philosophical Life, you shall not
fail.

STREPSIADES

Ladies, I'll tell you.

My ambition is modest, a trifling favor.
Just let my muscular tongue outrace the whole of Hellas
by a hundred laps.

KORYPHAIOS

Sir, you may consider your wishes granted.
Never, from this time forth, shall any politician in Athens
introduce more bills than you.

STREPSIADES

But I don't want to be a Senator!
Listen, ladies: all I want is to escape the clutches
of my creditors.

KORYPHAIOS

Your wishes are modest; we grant them.
And now, Candidate, boldly commit yourself to the hands
of our ministers.

STREPSIADES

Ladies, you've convinced me completely.
Anyway, thanks to my thoroughbreds, my son, and my wife,
I have no choice.

So I hereby bequeath you my body,
    for better, dear girls, or worse.
You can shrink me by slow starvation;
    or shrivel me dry with thirst.

You can freeze me or flay me skinless;
    thrash me as hard as you please.
Do any damn thing you've a mind to—
    my only conditions are these:

that when the ordeal is completed,
   a new Strepsiades rise,
renowned to the world as a WELSHER,
   famed as a TELLER OF LIES,

a CHEATER,
        a BASTARD,
               a PHONEY,
                     a BUM,
SHYSTER,
        MOUTHPIECE,
                TINHORN,
                     SCUM,
STOOLIE,
        CON-MAN,
                WINDBAG,
                     PUNK,
OILY,
        GREASY,
                HYPOCRITE,
                     SKUNK,
DUNGHILL,
        SQUEALER,
                SLIPPERY SAM,
FAKER,
        DIDDLER,
                SWINDLER,
                     SHAM,

—or just plain Lickspittle.

And then, dear ladies, for all I care,
   Science can have the body,
to experiment, as it sees fit,
   or serve me up as salami.

Yes, you can serve me up as salami!

KORYPHAIOS

Ah, here's a ready spirit, undaunted, unafraid!
                        —Sir,
complete your course with us and you shall win a glory
that towers to heaven.

STREPSIADES

Could you be a little more specific?

KORYPHAIOS

You shall pass your entire existence up in the air, among us,
strolling about with your head in the Clouds. Your life
shall be the envy of all mankind.

STREPSIADES

Ah, when shall I see that day?

KORYPHAIOS

Before long thousands of clients will stampede to your doors,
begging, pleading, imploring your service and advice
in all their lawsuits—many involving incredible sums.
I say no more.
       —And now, Sokrates, take this old candidate
and test his worthiness to undergo the solemn rites of initiation. Examine his mental powers; probe his mind and sift
him.

SOKRATES

Now then, tell me something about yourself.
The information is essential if I'm to know
what strategies to employ against you.

STREPSIADES

Strategies?
What do you think I am? A military objective?

SOKRATES

No. I'm merely attempting to ask a few questions.
First, is your memory keen?

STREPSIADES

Well, it is and it isn't.
If a man owes me money, I never seem to forget it.
But if I do the owing, I somehow never remember.

SOKRATES

Well, perhaps you have some talents for speaking?

STREPSIADES

No, no talent for talk. But for larceny, lots.

SOKRATES

But how can you possibly learn?

STREPSIADES

                                    Don't you worry.
I'll manage somehow.

SOKRATES

                        But look: suppose I toss you
some tidbit of higher wisdom? Could you catch it
on the fly?

STREPSIADES

          What do you take me for? A puppydog
snapping up wisdom?

SOKRATES

                    No, a beastly old ignoramus.
In fact, I'm afraid we'll have to whip our wisdom
into your hide.
                Hmmm.
                      Tell me, suppose someone
gave you a thrashing, what would you do?

STREPSIADES

                                          Why,
I'd take my thrashing. Then after a little while
I'd hunt up a witness, and then a little while later
I'd bring suit for Assault and Battery.

SOKRATES

                              All right, old man,
undress.

STREPSIADES

Undress? But why? Have I said something wrong?

SOKRATES

No, no. But we require all candidates for initiation
to strip naked.

STREPSIADES

But I'm not a burglar,* Sokrates.
Here, search me if you want.

SOKRATES

What do you think I am?
A policeman? This is a solemn philosophical initiation.
So stop your idiot blather and get undressed.

STREPSIADES

Starting to undress with extreme reluctance.

Oh, all right.
No, wait.
First answer me this. If I study very hard
and pay attention in class, which one of your students
will I look like?

SOKRATES

Why, you'll be the spitting image of—

Chairephon.

STREPSIADES

CHAIREPHON! But he's a walking cadaver.
I'll graduate a corpse.

He feverishly whisks his cloak back on.

SOKRATES

Damnation! Stop this stalling
and GET UNDRESSED!

*He pulls off Strepsiades' cloak and shoves him bodily
toward the black cavelike opening at the rear of
the Thinkery.*

Forward, Candidate!

STREPSIADES

NO! WAIT!
I'm scared Brr, it's as dark as a snakepit down there.
Give me a honeycake to throw to the snakes, Sokrates,
or they'll eat me alive.

SOKRATES

Forward, fool. No hesitation now!

*Sokrates shoves Strepsiades before him into the
opening at the rear of the Thinkery. Then he rushes
back, snatches up Strepsiades' discarded cloak.
smiles, tucks it under his tunic, and vanishes into
the Thinkery.*

CHORUS

Farewell, brave soul,
and may your future gleam as bright
as shines your courage now!
May all good fortune come to you
who, sunk in bitter age,
in the somber twilight of your years,
stride forth, undaunted, unafraid,
toward that uttermost frontier of thought
where wisdom lures you on,
O pioneer!

*The Chorus turns sharply and faces the audience.
From the wing appears the poet, the bald Aristophanes: he strides forth and addresses the audience
directly.*

ARISTOPHANES*

Gentlemen, in the name of Dionysos to whom I owe my
    nurture as a poet,
I intend to confront you with my personal complaints,
    frankly and freely,
as a poet should.

My ambitions, of course, are very simply
stated:
the First Prize and a reputation for talent and wit.

Accordingly,
firmly convinced that this audience was composed of men
of taste,
and that this play, *The Clouds*, was the finest of my comedies to date,
I submitted an earlier version, expecting your pleasure and
approval.
It cost me enormous anguish and labor, and yet I was forced
to withdraw,
ignobly defeated by cheap and vulgar rivals. My present
reproaches,
needless to say, are aimed at those self-styled critics and wits
for whom this revision has been made.

However, to the men
of true taste
among you, I say this: I am, as always, your faithful friend,
and never will I willingly or knowingly abandon you or
reproach you.
After all, I still remember that glorious day when the
Judges—
men of whose extraordinary taste and discrimination it is a
joy to speak—
awarded the First Prize to my youthful comedy, *The Banqueters*.
Now at that time, gentlemen, my Muse was the merest slip
of a girl,
a tender virgin who could not—without outraging all propriety—
give birth. So I exposed her child, her maiden effort, and a
stranger
rescued the foundling.* But it was you, gentlemen, whose
generous patronage
nourished my offspring, and I have never since doubted
those tokens
of your exquisite taste.

And now, gentlemen, like Elektra in
the play,*
a sister-comedy comes in search of you today, hoping to find
those same tokens of recognition. Let her so much as
glimpse

a single curl from her brother's head, and she will know
　her own,
as I shall know the tokens of your approval.

　　　　　　　　　　　　　　　She's a dainty
　play.
Observe, gentlemen, her natural modesty, the demureness of
　her dress,
with no dangling thong of leather,* red and thick at the tip,
to make the small boys snigger. Note too her delicate refine-
　ment—
her refusal to indulge in cheap cracks at the expense of
　baldness,
and the quiet dignity of her dancing, with nothing salacious
　about it.
Observe the absence of farcical slapstick and sensational
　situations.
Here you see no poor old man drubbing his opponents with
　a stick
in a futile attempt to hide the abysmal poverty of his verses.
Nor does she fling herself on stage with tragic torches
　blazing
and bloodcurdling fustian. No, gentlemen, my comedy
　comes to you
relying upon herself and her poetry.

　　　　　　　　　　　　　This is what she is,
and I am the poet, her adoring father. Now I may be bald-
　headed
(as some of my competitors so tirelessly point out), but I
　am *not* vapid;
and it has never been *my* practice to serve you up some
　réchauffé
of stale and tired plots. No, my fictions are always fresh,
no two of them the least alike, and all of them uproariously
　funny.
Observe, moreover, gentlemen, that it was *I* who punched
　Kleon
in the paunch in his hour of pride; yet once I had him on
　the ground,
I refused to kick him.

　　　　　　　　　　But consider my competitors; note
　their conduct
with poor Hyperbolos. Once they had him floored, they
　never stopped

grinding him down in the dirt—*plus* his mother into the bargain.

It was Eupolis, of course, who led the mass-attack upon Hyperbolos;

he gutted my *Knights*, botched it, and then dragged the resultant abortion

on stage—a stunning new plagiarism entitled (of *course*) *The Pederast.*

Even as larceny, a complete flop: Eupolis wanted a dirty dance,*

so what did he do but introduce a drunken old hag to shake her hips?

Not that *she* was original either; he lifted her from an ancient play

by Phrynichos (who quite sensibly fed the old bitch to a sea monster).

So much for Eupolis.

> After him, Hermippos opened up on Hyperbolos,

and before long every imitator in town was after Hyperbolos' hide,

and every last one of them plagiarized my celebrated simile on the eels.*

I devoutly pray that those who like such stuff are bored to death

by mine. But as for you men of taste who enjoy your Aristophanes

and applaud his talent, why, posterity will endorse your judgment.

Exit Aristophanes.

CHORUS

> You, our king, we summon first.
> Omnipotence, in glory throned,
> look down upon our dances.
> > *O Zeus, be with us now!*

> And you, steward of the sea,
> whose savage trident's power
> heaves the shattered world
> and pries the waters up,
> > *O Poseidon, hear our prayer!*

And you, O Father Ether,
pure presence of Air,
nourisher, sustainer,
   O Spirit, quicken us now!

And you whose flaring horses blaze
across the skies! O benison,
splendor whose shining spills
on earth, on heaven,
   O Light, illuminate us all!

KORYPHAIOS

Gentlemen, Critics, and Clever Fellows:
        YOUR ATTENTION
 PLEASE.
Because our agenda includes a few complaints and home truths,
we shall be blunt.
     WE ARE TIRED OF BEING IGNORED.
Of all the gods
     to whom this city stands in debt for benefits
 conferred,
no god has brought more benefits than we. Yet we alone,
forsaken and forgotten gods, receive no sacrifice at all.
But surely we need not remind you of all our loving care,
the unsleeping devotion lavished, gentlemen, on your behalf?
   For example,
whenever you launch some exceptionally crack-brained
 project,
we promptly thunder our objection; we drizzle our dis-
 pleasure.
Or look to recent history. Have you forgotten that black day
when a low tanner, a repulsive atheist nicknamed Paphlagon*
was running for election as General? And how we re-
 sponded?
How we furrowed our beetling brows and rumbled with
 rage,
and *hard on the heels of the Levin rattled the steeds of
 Thunder?*
How the moon, in dudgeon, snuffed her flame amongst the
 rack,

and the sun in sullenness withdrew,* curling his blazing wick
back beneath his globe, refusing to shine if this Kleon
were elected?
                    So you elected—Kleon!
                                        As native Athenians,
    gentlemen,
you are all familiar with that local brand of statesmanship
sometimes known as Blundering Through—the curious be-
    lief
which holds that, by virtue of some timely divine interven-
    tion,
all your most appalling political blunders will sooner or later
redound to the interest of Athens.
                              Whence the question arises:
why not make a good thing of this latest glaring example
of Blundering Through?
                    How?
                          By convicting this cormorant
    Kleon
of bribery and peculation. Then muzzle his omnivorous
    maw
and slap a yoke around his neck. Not only is such action
in perfect accord with your long tradition of Blundering
    Through,
but with one shrewd stroke all your bungling is redeemed
as statesmanship, manifestly furthering the noblest interests
    of Athens.

CHORUS

> O lord of Delos, you
> who haunt the cliffs and scarp,
> where the ridge of Kynthos rises,
> > *O Phoibos, be with us now!*

> And you of Ephesos, lady,
> glory of the shrine of gold
> where the Lydian women worship,
> > *O Artemis, come to the dance!*

> And you, goddess on the hill,
> mistress of this lovely land
> beneath your aegis guarded,
> > *O Athene, be with us now!*

And you, dancer of Delphoi,
runner upon the peaks, at dark
when the trailing torches flicker
and the whirling Maenads cry their joy,
    O Dionysos, dance with us now!

KORYPHAIOS

Our cluster of Clouds had gathered for the outing down to
    Athens
when we chanced to run into the Moon, who asked us to
    deliver
the following message on her behalf:
                                GREETINGS SALU-
    TATIONS ETCET
TO ATHENS AND ALLIES STOP MY DEITY MOR-
    TALLY OFFENDED
BY YOUR SCANDALOUS RUDENESS DESPITE
    MANY SUBSTANTIAL CONTRIBUTIONS
TO WELFARE OF ATHENS STOP AM WOMAN OF
    ACTIONS REPEAT ACTIONS
NOT WORDS
            (Signed)
                THE MOON.
                                And the Moon has a
    point, gentlemen.
Thanks to her shining efforts on your behalf, your average
    savings
on lighting alone run more than a drachma a month. Why,
I can hear you now, instructing your slaves as you leave the
    house,
"No need to buy torches tonight, lad. The moonlight's
    lovely."
And moonlight is merely one of her many services.
    Nonetheless,
you brusquely refuse to devise an Accurate Lunar Calendar,
and your month is a consequent chaos,* a masterpiece of
    temporal confusion.
Worse still, when the gods come hungrily trudging home at
    night
and find they must do without their dinner because you
    celebrate
your festivals on the wrong day, it's the poor innocent Moon

who bears the brunt of their heavenly grumbling. What's
    more,
on the days when you ought to sacrifice to the gods, you're
    bustling
about holding trials or torturing some poor witness on the
    rack.
And conversely, no sooner do the gods fast or go into
    mourning
for Memnon or Sarpedon, than you Athenians start
    carousing
and boozing.
            So be warned, gentlemen.
                        Very recently the gods
stripped Hyperbolos of his seat* on the Commission for
    Public Festivals
and Other Red-Letter Days—a measure designed to teach
    him
and all such Johnnies-Come-Lately a little respect for time.

*While the Chorus resumes its customary position,
the doors of the Thinkery are thrown open and
Sokrates appears.*

SOKRATES

Almighty Effluvium! Ozone and Chaos! Never
in all my days have I seen such peerless stupidity,
such a bungling, oblivious, brainless imbecile as this!
I no sooner teach him the merest snippets of science
than he suffers an attack of total amnesia. Still,
the Truth is my mistress and I obey.

*He goes to the Thinkery door and peers into the
darkness.*

                        —Strepsiades,
where are you?
             Fetch your mattress and come outside.

*Strepsiades appears at the door, tugging at his
mattress.*

STREPSIADES

I can't come. The little bugs won't let me leave.

SOKRATES

Down with it, blockhead. Now your attention, please.

STREPSIADES

Ready.

SOKRATES

      To resume then, what particular discipline
in that vast array of choices offered by your ignorance
would you especially like to acquire? For instance,
would you prefer diction or rhythm or measures?

STREPSIADES

                                    Measures.
Why, just the other day the flourman swindled me
of half a peck.

SOKRATES

                Not dry measures, dunderhead!
I want to know which *meter* you'd prefer to master—
trimeter or tetrameter.

STREPSIADES

                Well, I like the yard
as well as anything.

SOKRATES

                Rubbish. Palpable rubbish.

STREPSIADES

What would you like to bet that your trimeter isn't
exactly three feet?

SOKRATES

             Why, you illiterate numskull!
However, perhaps you'd do better with rhythm.

STREPSIADES

                           Rhythm?
Will rhythm buy the groceries?

SOKRATES

Sensitivity to rhythm
confers a certain ineluctable social *savoir-faire*.
Polite society will accept you if you can discriminate, say,
between the marital anapest and common dactylic—
sometimes vulgarly called finger-rhythm.*

STREPSIADES

Finger-rhythm?
I know *that*.

SOKRATES

Define it then.

STREPSIADES

Extending his middle finger in an obscene gesture.

Why, it's tapping time
with *this* finger. Of course, when I was a boy—

*Raising his phallus to the ready.**

I used to make rhythm with *this* one.

SOKRATES

Why, you lout!

STREPSIADES

But look, you goose, I don't want to learn this stuff.

SOKRATES

Then what *do* you want to learn?

STREPSIADES

Logic! Logic!
Teach me your Immoral Logic!

SOKRATES

But, my dear fellow,
one must begin by mastering the rudiments of language.
For instance, can you list me the male quadrupeds?

STREPSIADES

Pooh, I *would* be a damnfool if I didn't know *them*.
Listen: the ram, the buck, the stallion, the bull,
the duck—

SOKRATES

And now the females of the same quadrupeds.

STREPSIADES

Let's see: the ewe, the doe, the mare, the cow,
the duck—

SOKRATES

Stop right there. A gross solecism.
According to you, the word *duck* apparently applies
to both the male and female of the species.

STREPSIADES

Huh?
How do you mean?

SOKRATES

In *your* usage, they're both ducks.

STREPSIADES

Holy Poseidon, you're right! What should I have said?

SOKRATES

The male is a *duck;* the female's a *duchess.**

STREPSIADES

A *duchess?*
Bravo! Almighty Ozone, that's a good one!
For that little lesson, you can bring out your basket
and I'll fill it with seed.

SOKRATES

Oops. Another solecism.
You've made *basket* masculine, when it's feminine.*

STREPSIADES

What?

Basket is masculine? But why?

SOKRATES

Because the ending *-et*
is what in grammar we call a masculine termination.
Like the *-os* ending of *Kleonymos*.

STREPSIADES

Wait. I don't see.

SOKRATES

I repeat: *basket* and *Kleonymos* are masculine in form
and ending.

STREPSIADES

Kleonymos *masculine*? But *he*'s feminine.
Form and ending. Queer as they come.

But look,
what *should* I call a basket?

SOKRATES

Why, a *baskette*, of course.
By analogy with *toilette*.

STREPSIADES

Baskette, eh?

SOKRATES

That's it.
Now you're talking Greek.

STREPSIADES

The *baskette* of *Kleonymette*?

SOKRATES

Precisely. Which brings us to the distinction between
men's names and women's names.

STREPSIADES

Oh, I know the female names.

SOKRATES

For example?

STREPSIADES

For example: Lysilla, Philinna, Demetria,
Kleitagora—

SOKRATES

And now recite some masculine names.

STREPSIADES

Easy. There's thousands of them. Like Philoxenos, Melesias,
Amynias—

SOKRATES

Stop, you nincompoop. I asked for men's names,
not women's names.

STREPSIADES

You mean those *aren't* men's names?

SOKRATES

Not men's names at all. A transparent confusion
between singular and plural. Suppose, for instance,
we drop the plural *s* from Amynias, what would we have?

STREPSIADES

Why, Amynia.*

SOKRATES

You see, by dropping the plural *s*,
you've made Amynias a singular woman.

STREPSIADES

Well, the draftdodger,
it serves him right. But why am I learning stuff
any damn fool knows?

SOKRATES

Fool, you flatter yourself.
However, lie down on your mattress and—

STREPSIADES

And what, Sokrates?

SOKRATES

And lucubrate upon your dilemma.

STREPSIADES

Please, no, Sokrates!
Anywhere but there. Couldn't I just go and lubricate
on the ground?

SOKRATES

Permission refused.

STREPSIADES

Ohh, what a fate!
Those little bugs are sure to crucify me now.

*Strepsiades burrows under the infested sheepskins
on his mattress, while Sokrates chants encouragement.*

SOKRATES

First concentrate.
Then cerebrate.
  Now concentrate again.

Then lucubrate.
Next, speculate.
  Now ruminate. And then,

if your mind gets stuck,
don't curse your luck.
  Get up! Quick as a wink,

cut through the knot,
swift as a thought,
  but THINK, Candidate, THINK!

Now hence, ye Syrops of Sleep! Come hither, O Pain!

STREPSIADES

Yooooooow! Yooooooow!

SOKRATES

Look here, what's biting you now?

STREPSIADES

Biting, you say?
THEY'RE MURDERING ME!
Out of the ticking
the bugs come creeping.
They're biting my ribs.
They're swilling my blood.
My balls are all sores.
My ass is a shambles.
THEY'RE MURDERING ME!

SOKRATES

There, there, old fellow. Don't take it so hard.

STREPSIADES

DON'T TAKE IT SO HARD?
When my money's gone?
When my skin's gone?
When my blood's gone?
And then what's more,
when I tried to hum
and forget these bites,
I DAMN NEAR DIED!

*There is a brief interval of silence during which
Strepsiades hums and thrashes under his covers.
Then Sokrates picks up a sheepskin and peers under.*

SOKRATES

Here, what's this? Have you stopped lucubrating?

STREPSIADES

Who, *me?*

By Poseidon, I *have not!*

SOKRATES

What thoughts have you had?

STREPSIADES

Only this: I've been thinking how much of me would be
left when the bugs got through.

SOKRATES

Bah! Consume you for an ass.

STREPSIADES

I *am* consumed.

SOKRATES

Courage, gaffer. We mustn't repine.
Pull back your covers and concentrate. What we need
is some clever quibbling subterfuge with which to frustrate
and fleece your creditors.

STREPSIADES

Who's fleecing *who*, Sokrates?
That's what I'd like to know.

Another brief silence follows.

SOKRATES

Hmmm. I wonder
what he's up to now? I'll peek under the covers.

He lifts the sheepskin.

What's this? Asleep on the job, are you?

STREPSIADES

By Apollo,
I'm *not* sleeping!

SOKRATES

Any thoughts yet?

STREPSIADES

Not a thing.

SOKRATES

Surely you've found *something*.

STREPSIADES

Well, only this thing
I've got in my hand.

SOKRATES

Buffoon! Get back to your pallet
and cogitate.

STREPSIADES

But, Sokrates, what am I cogitating *about*?

SOKRATES

A moot question, friend, whose answer lies with you.
When *you* know what *you* want, kindly illuminate *me*.

STREPSIADES

But I've told you ten thousand times already, Sokrates.
It's my debts. I want to welsh on my debts.

SOKRATES

Splendid.
Then back to your pallet.

Strepsiades dutifully crawls under his sheepskin.

And now distill your mind
to its airiest essence, allowing the subtle elixirs of thought
to permeate and penetrate every pore of the problem.
Then Analyze, Refine, Synthesize, Define—

STREPSIADES

Frantically thrashing to escape the bugs.

OUCH!

SOKRATES

Stop fidgeting!
        —However, in the case of a dilemma,
defer your inquiry briefly. When refreshed, return,
sift your conclusions and knead vigorously. Then mull
the results.

STREPSIADES

Suddenly illuminated.

                Ooooh, Sokrates!

SOKRATES

                                Yes?

STREPSIADES

                                EUREKA!
I've got it. A glorious dodge for ditching my debts!

SOKRATES

Aha. Expatiate.

STREPSIADES

                Well, just suppose—

SOKRATES

                                Supposing *what?*

STREPSIADES

Just suppose I rented one of those witchwomen from
Thessaly* and ordered her to charm down the moon from
the sky. And then I snatch up the moon and I pop her into
a box, and polish her face until she shines like a mirror.

SOKRATES

And what would you gain by that?

STREPSIADES

                        What would I gain?
Why, think what would happen if the moon never rose.
I wouldn't have to pay interest.

SOKRATES

No interest? But why?

STREPSIADES

Because interest falls due on the last day of the month,
before the New Moon, doesn't it?

SOKRATES

A superlative swindle!
Now then, let me propose a somewhat thornier case.
You are threatened, we assume, with a suit for five talents.
Problem: how do you quash the verdict?

STREPSIADES

How? *I* don't know.
I'd have to meditate on *that*.

SOKRATES

By all means meditate;
but beware of immuring your mind with excessive intro-
spection. Allow your intellect instead to sally forth upon
her own, as though you held a cockroach on a leash.

STREPSIADES

Suddenly illuminated.

Ooh, Sokrates, I've found a glorious bamboozle! I've got it!
Admit it, it's wonderful!

SOKRATES

Kindly expound it first.

STREPSIADES

Well, have you ever noticed in the druggists' shops
that beautiful stone, that transparent sort of glass
that makes things burn?

SOKRATES

A magnifying glass, you mean?

STREPSIADES

That's it. Well, suppose I'm holding one of these,
and while the court secretary is recording my case,
I stand way off, keeping the sun behind me,
and scorch out every word of the charges.*

SOKRATES

                                        By the Graces,

a magnificent bamboozle!

STREPSIADES

                              Whew, and am I glad
to get *that* suit quashed!

SOKRATES

                              Now then, try your teeth
on this little teaser.

STREPSIADES

                    Shoot.

SOKRATES

                              This time imagine
that you find yourself a defendant without a witness.
Your case is absolutely hopeless. Problem: to prevent
your opponent's suit from coming to trial.

STREPSIADES

                                              Pooh,
nothing to it at all.

SOKRATES

                    Elaborate.

STREPSIADES

                              But it's a pushover,
Sokrates. While they were trying the case before mine,
I'd go hang myself.

SOKRATES

Preposterous!

STREPSIADES

It's *not* preposterous.
You can't sue a corpse.

SOKRATES

Poppycock. Palpable rubbish.
As your tutor, I hereby resign. And now, GET OUT!

STREPSIADES

You resign? But why?

Falling on his knees in supplication.

Oh, please. I implore you, Sokrates . . .

SOKRATES

But you forget everything as fast as you learn it, numskull!
Tell me, what was the first lesson?
Well, speak up.

STREPSIADES

Let me think.
The first lesson?
The *first* lesson?
Ummm. That whoozit you put seeds in!
For god's sake,
what *is* it called?

SOKRATES

Why, you blithering bungler!
You senile incompetent! You . . . you mooncalf! Clear out!

STREPSIADES

Sweet gods in heaven, what's to become of me now?
I'm a goner unless I master those sleights-of-tongue.

Falling on his knees before the Chorus.

O most gracious Clouds, please advise me. Tell me
what to do.

KORYPHAIOS

Our counsel, reverend sir, is this.
Have you a grown-up son perhaps? Then send him off
to study in your place.

STREPSIADES

It's true, ladies, I have a son,
but he's a gentleman, you see, with a true gentleman's
natural distaste for learning. So what can I do?

KORYPHAIOS

Is he the boss?

STREPSIADES

Well, he's a strapping, sturdy boy,
and there's a bit of eagle-blood on his mother's side.
Still, I'll go fetch him anyway. If he refuses
to learn his lessons, by god, he'll never set foot
in my house again!

To Sokrates.

—I won't be gone a moment.

Exit Strepsiades into his house.

CHORUS

Now, sir, you see
what blessings we,
    the Clouds, have brought to pass.

E.g. this fool-
ish, willing tool,
    this frantic, eager ass.

But seize your prey.
Avoid delay.
    No matter how well hooked,

                    your fish is not
                    fried fish till caught—
                        and goose is better cooked.

Exit Sokrates. Enter Strepsiades, dragging
Pheidippides.

STREPSIADES

Out with you! By Condensation, you won't stay here!
Go cut your teeth on Megakles' money!

PHEIDIPPIDES

                                    But Father,
what's the matter with you? Are you out of your head?
Almighty Zeus, you must be mad!

STREPSIADES

                                "Almighty Zeus!"
What musty rubbish! Imagine, a boy your age.
still believing in Zeus!

PHEIDIPPIDES

                    What's so damn funny?

STREPSIADES

It tickles me when the heads of toddlers like you
are still stuffed with such outdated notions. Now then,
listen to me and I'll tell you a secret or two
that might make an intelligent man of you yet.
But remember: you mustn't breathe a word of this.

PHEIDIPPIDES

A word of what?

STREPSIADES

                    Didn't you just swear by Zeus?

PHEIDIPPIDES

I did.

STREPSIADES

Now learn what Education can do for *you:*
Pheidippides, there is no Zeus.

PHEIDIPPIDES

There is no Zeus?

STREPSIADES

No Zeus. Convection-Principle's in power now.
Zeus has been banished.

PHEIDIPPIDES

Drivel!

STREPSIADES

Take my word for it,
it's absolutely true.

PHEIDIPPIDES

Who says so?

STREPSIADES

Sokrates.
And Chairephon too. The famous expert on fleafeet.

PHEIDIPPIDES

Are you so far gone on the road to complete insanity
you'd believe the word of those charlatans?

STREPSIADES

Hush, boy.
For shame. I won't hear you speaking disrespectfully
of such eminent scientists and geniuses. And, what's more,
men of such fantastic frugality and Spartan thrift,
they regard baths, haircuts, and personal cleanliness
generally as an utter waste of time and money—whereas
you, dear boy, have taken me to the cleaner's so many times,
I'm damn near washed up. Come on, for your father's sake,
go and learn.

PHEIDIPPIDES

What do they teach that's worth knowing?

STREPSIADES

Worth knowing? Why, the accumulated wisdom of mankind.
For instance, what a blockhead and numskull you are.
Hmmm.
Wait here. I'll be right back.

Strepsiades darts into his house.

PHEIDIPPIDES

Gods in heaven,
what should I do? My father's gone completely balmy.
Should I hale him into court on charges of insanity
or notify the undertakers?

*Strepsiades reappears with a pair of ducks. He holds
up first one and then the other.*

STREPSIADES

Now then, what's this called?

PHEIDIPPIDES

That? A duck.

STREPSIADES

Excellent. Now what do you call this?

PHEIDIPPIDES

Why, another duck.

STREPSIADES

Another duck? You stupid boy.
From now on you must learn to call them by their right
names. This one is a duck; that one's a duchess.

PHEIDIPPIDES

A *duchess!*
So this is the glorious wisdom you've picked up
from those walking corpses!

STREPSIADES

>   Oh, there's lots more too,
> but I'm so old everything I learn goes in one ear
> and right out the other.

PHEIDIPPIDES

>   Ah. Doubtless that explains
> how you lost your cloak.

STREPSIADES

>   I didn't lose it. I swapped it.
> For thoughts.

PHEIDIPPIDES

>   And where have your sandals gone, you idiot?

STREPSIADES

> In the words of Perikles himself when they asked him
> where the money went: *Expended as required.*
> *No comment.**
>   And now, inside with you, boy.
> Humor me in this and you can make an ass of yourself
> in any way you like. Ah, how well I remember those days
> when you were six, and I had to humor your tantrums.
> Why, the very first pay I ever drew as a juror
> went to buy you a cart at the fair.

PHEIDIPPIDES

>   All right, Dad.
> But someday you'll be sorry.

STREPSIADES

>   Ah, good dutiful boy.
> —Hallo there, Sokrates!
>   Hey, Sokrates, come outside.
> I've brought my son along—no damn thanks to him.

Enter Sokrates from the Thinkery.

SOKRATES

Why, he's still a baby. How could a toddler like this
possibly operate our Hanging Baskets?

PHEIDIPPIDES

As for you,
why don't you hang yourself and skip the basket?

STREPSIADES

Here,
for shame! You'd insult the Master?

SOKRATES

Imitating Pheidippides.

"Thkip the bathket."
Dear me, what adorable, childish prattle. And look
at those great sulking lower lips. How in the world
could this fumbling foetus ever master the arts
of Verdict-Quashing, False Witness, Innuendo,
and Character Assassination? On the other hand, however,
the case is not without precedent. *Even* Hyperbolos,*
after all, somehow mastered the tricks of the trade.
The fee, of course, was prodigious.

STREPSIADES

Now don't you worry,
Sokrates. The boy's a born philosopher. Yes, sir,
when he was just a mite of a shaver, *so* high,
he used to make the cleverest things you ever saw.
Why, there were dollhouses, sailboats, little pushcarts
from scraps of leather, and the sweetest little frogs
carved from fruit peel. He's a scholar, all right.
So tutor him in your two logics—traditional Philosophical
Logic and that flashy modern sophistic logic they call
Immoral because it's so wonderfully wicked. In any case,
if he can't master both logics, I insist that he learn the
Immoral Kind of argument.

SOKRATES

Philosophy and Sophistry*
will instruct your son in person. And now, gentlemen,
if you'll excuse me, I must leave.

STREPSIADES

But remember, Sokrates:
I want him able to make an utter mockery of the truth.

*Exit Sokrates. After his departure the doors of the Thinkery
are thrown open and Philosophy and Sophistry are rolled forward in great gilded cages. From the shoulders down, both are
human; from the neck up they are fighting-cocks.* Philosophy
(or the Traditional Logic) is a large, muscular rooster, powerful
but not heavy, expressing in his movements that inward harmony and grace and dignity which the Old Education was
meant to produce; his plumage is so simple and dignified as
to seem almost dingy. Sophistry, by contrast, is comparatively
slight, with sloping shoulders, an emaciated pallor, an enormous
tongue and a disproportionately large phallus. His body is
graceless but extremely quick-moving; his every motion ex-
presses defiant belligerence, and his plumage is brilliant to the
point of flashiness. The debate itself should be conducted at
top speed with much scratching and spurring. As the Attend-
ants open the cages, the fighters step out and circle each other
warily, jockeying for position.*

PHILOSOPHY

Front and center, you Feathered Impertinence.
Take your little bow before the audience.
You like to swagger.

SOPHISTRY

Why, you Pompous Lump,
with all my heart. The bigger the crowd,
the better I'll rebut you.

PHILOSOPHY

You'll rebut *me?*
Who are *you*, runt?

SOPHISTRY

A Logic.

PHILOSOPHY

You,
A Logic? Why, you cheap, stunted Loquacity!
You pipsqueak Palaver!

SOPHISTRY

I may be called
Mere Sophistry, but I'll chop you down
to size. I'll *refute* you.

PHILOSOPHY

Refute *me?* How?

SOPHISTRY

With unconventionality. With ultramodernity.
With unorthodox ideas.

PHILOSOPHY

For whose present vogue
we are indebted to this audience of imbeciles
and asses.

SOPHISTRY

Asses? These sophisticated gentlemen?
These wits?

PHILOSOPHY

I'll *invalidate* you.

SOPHISTRY

Invalidate *me?*
How, fossil?

PHILOSOPHY

My arguments are Truth and Justice.

SOPHISTRY

Then I'll disarm you and defeat you, friend.
Your Justice doesn't exist.

PHILOSOPHY

What? No Justice?

Preposterous!

SOPHISTRY

Then show it to me. Where is it?

PHILOSOPHY

Where is Justice? Why, in the Lap of the Gods.

SOPHISTRY

In the Lap of the Gods? Then would you explain
how Zeus escaped punishment after he imprisoned
his father?* The inconsistency is glaring.

PHILOSOPHY

Aaaagh.

What nauseating twaddle. It turns my stomach.

SOPHISTRY

Why, you Decrepitude! You Doddering Dotard!

PHILOSOPHY

Why,

you Precocious Pederast! You Palpable Pervert!

SOPHISTRY

Pelt me with roses!

PHILOSOPHY

You Toadstool! O Cesspool!

SOPHISTRY

Wreath my hair with lilies!

PHILOSOPHY

Why, you Parricide!

SOPHISTRY

Shower me with gold! Look, don't you see
I welcome your abuse?

PHILOSOPHY

Welcome it, monster?
In my day we would have cringed with shame.

SOPHISTRY

Whereas *now* we're flattered. Times change.
The vices of your age are stylish today.

PHILOSOPHY

Repulsive Whippersnapper!

SOPHISTRY

Disgusting Fogy!

PHILOSOPHY

Because of *you* the schools of Athens
stand deserted; one whole generation
chaffers in the streets, gaping and idle.
Mark my words: someday this city
shall learn what you have made her men:
effeminates and fools.

SOPHISTRY

Ugh, you're squalid!

PHILOSOPHY

Whereas you've become a Dandy and a Fop!
But I remember your beggared beginnings,
playing as Telephos,* grubby and shifty,
tricked out in Euripidean rags and tatters

and cramming your wallet with moldy leavings
from Pandaletos' loaf.*

SOPHISTRY

What a prodigy of wisdom
was there!

PHILOSOPHY

And what a prodigy of madness here—
your madness, and madder still than you,
this maddened city which lets you live—
you, corrupter and destroyer of her youth!

SOPHISTRY

Throwing a wing about Pheidippides.

Why, you Hoary Fossil! This is one student
you'll never teach!

PHILOSOPHY

Pulling Pheidippides back.

Teach him I *shall*—
unless he's prepared to devote his career
exclusively to drivel.

SOPHISTRY

Bah, rave to yourself.
—Come here, boy.

PHILOSOPHY

You touch him at your peril.

KORYPHAIOS

Intervening.

Gentlemen, forego your wrangling and abuse,
and each present his arguments in turn.
Describe how *you* taught the men of the past,
and *you*, Sir, your New Education.

PHILOSOPHY

                              I second
your proposal.

SOPHISTRY

              As do I.

KORYPHAIOS

                    Excellent.
Who will speak first?

SOPHISTRY

                    Let him begin.
I yield the floor. But when he's done,
I'll smother him beneath so huge
a driving hail of Modern Thought
and Latest Views, he cannot speak—
or if he does, my hornet words
and waspish wit will sting him so,
he'll never speak again.

CHORUS
—At last!
            —The Great Debate begins!
                              —Between these two
contending, clever speakers,
                    —matched so fairly,
                              —who
will win, is anybody's guess.
                    —Both are subtle,
—both facile, both witty,
                    —both masters of rebuttal
—and abuse.
            —The stake? Wisdom.
                              —Wisdom is the prize.
—For her they fight.
                    —For her their rival hackles rise.
—So listen well.
            —Upon their skill, the destinies of Lan-
guage, Intellect, and Educated Athens hang.

KORYPHAIOS

To Philosophy.

Come, Sir, I summon you—you who conferred your crown
of virtue upon the Older Generation—to take the stand. Be
bold; rise and with clarion tongue tell us what you represent.

PHILOSOPHY

                                                    Gentlemen,
I propose to speak of the Old Education,* as it flourished
    once
beneath my tutelage, when Homespun Honesty, Plainspeak-
    ing, and Truth
were still honored and practiced, and throughout the schools
    of Athens
the regime of the three D's—DISCIPLINE, DECORUM,
    and DUTY—
enjoyed unchallenged supremacy.
                                    Our curriculum was
    Music and Gymnastic,
enforced by that rigorous discipline summed up in the old
    adage:
BOYS SHOULD BE SEEN BUT NOT HEARD. This was
    our cardinal rule,
and when the students, mustered by groups according to
    region,
were marched in squads to school, discipline and absolute
silence prevailed.
                        Ah, they were hardy, manly youngsters. Why,
even on winter mornings when the snow, like powdered
    chaff,
came sifting down, their only protection against the bitter
    weather
was a thin and scanty tunic. In the classes, posture was
    stressed
and the decencies firmly enforced: the students stood in
    rows,
rigidly at attention, while the master rehearsed them by rote,
over and over. The music itself was traditional and
    standard—
such familiar anthems and hymns as those, for instance,
    beginning

A Voice from Afar or *Hail, O Pallas, Destroyer!**—and the
old modes
were strictly preserved in all their austere and simple beauty.
Clowning in class was sternly forbidden, and those who
improvised
or indulged in those fantastic flourishes and trills so much in
vogue
with the degenerate, effeminate school of Phrynis, were
promptly thrashed
for subverting the Muses.

                        In the gymnasium too decorum
was demanded.
The boys were seated together, stripped to the skin, on the
bare ground,
keeping their legs thrust forward, shyly screening their
nakedness
from the gaze of the curious. Why, so modest were students
then,
that when they rose, they carefully smoothed out the ground
beneath them,
lest even a pair of naked buttocks leaving its trace in the
sand
should draw the eyes of desire. Anointing with oil was
forbidden
below the line of the navel, and consequently their genitals
kept
their boyish bloom intact and the quincelike freshness of
youth.
Toward their lovers their conduct was manly*: you didn't
see *them*.
mincing or strutting, or prostituting themselves with girlish
voices
or coy, provocative glances.

                        At table courtesy and good
manners
were compulsory. Not a boy of that generation would have
dreamed
of taking so much as a radish or the merest pinch of parsley
before his elders had been served. Rich foods were
prohibited,
raucous laughter or crossing their legs forbidden. . . .

SOPHISTRY

Ugh,

what musty, antiquated rubbish. It reeks of golden grass-
hoppers,
all gewgaws and decaying institutions!

PHILOSOPHY

Nonetheless, these

were the precepts
on which I bred a generation of heroes, the men who fought
at Marathon.

To Sophistry.

And what do *you* teach?

Modesty?

No, vanity

and softness,
and the naked beauty of the body muffled in swirling clothes
gross and unmanly. Why, at Panathenaia now it sickens me
to see the boys dancing, ashamed of their own bodies,
effetely forgetting their duty to the goddess while they screen
their nakedness behind their shields.

Bah.

To Pheidippides.

No, young man, by your courage

I challenge you. Turn your back upon his blandishments of
vice,
the rotten law courts and the cheap, corrupting softness of
the baths.
Choose instead the Old, the Philosophical Education. Follow
me
and from my lips acquire the virtues of a man:—

A sense of

shame,
that decency and innocence of mind that shrinks from doing
wrong.
To feel the true man's blaze of anger when his honor is
provoked.

Deference toward one's elders; respect for one's father and
   mother.
To preserve intact, unsullied by disgrace or stained with
   wrong,
that image of Manliness and Modesty by which alone you
   live.
Purity:—to avoid the brothels and the low, salacious leer
of prostituted love—which, being bought, corrupts your
   manhood
and destroys your name. Toward your father scrupulous
   obedience;
to honor his declining years who spent his prime in rearing
   you.
Not to call him Dotard or Fogy—

SOPHISTRY

                         Boy, if you follow his
advice, you'll finish by looking like one of Hippokrates'
sissified sons. They'll call *you* Mollycoddle Milksop.

PHILOSOPHY

                         Rubbish. I promise
   you,
not contentious disputations and the cheap, courtroom cant
of this flabby, subpoena-serving, shyster-jargoned
   de-generation,
but true athletic prowess, the vigor of contending manhood
in prime perfection of physique, muscular and hard, glowing
with health.
            Ah, I can see you now, as through an idyl
   moving—
you with some companion of your age, modest and manly
   like you,
strolling by Akademe perhaps, or there among the olives,
sprinting side by side together, crowned with white reed,
breathing with every breath the ecstasy of Spring returning,
the sudden fragrance of the season's leisure, the smell of
   woodbine
and the catkins flung by the poplar, while touching
   overhead,

the leaves of the linden and plane rustle, in love, together.
So follow me, young man, and win perfection of physique.
   To wit—

Demonstrating each attribute individually.

> BUILD, Stupendous.
> COMPLEXION, Splendid.
> SHOULDERS, Gigantic.
> TONGUE, Petite.
> BUTTOCKS, Brawny.
> PECKER, Discreet.

But follow my opponent here, and your reward shall be, as
   follows:

> BUILD, Effeminate.
> COMPLEXION, Ghastly.
> SHOULDERS, Hunched.
> TONGUE, Enormous.
> BUTTOCKS, Flabby.
> PECKER, Preposterous!

(But thereby insuring you an enormous and devoted political
   following.)
What is worse, you shall learn to make a mockery of all
   morality,
systematically confounding good with evil and evil with
   good,
so plumped and pursy with villainy, sodomy, disgrace, and
   perversion,
you resemble ANTIMACHOS himself.
                              Depravity can sink

   no lower.

CHORUS

—Bravo!
         —What brilliance!
                  —What finesse!
                           —*This* is wisdom
at its noble best!
         —Such Modesty,
                  —such Decorum
in every lovely word distilled!
                  —Ah, lucky they

—whose happy lives were lived
                              —beneath your dispensa-
tion,
        —by all the ancient virtues blessed!

To Sophistry.

                                        —So, sir,
—despite your vaunted subtlety and wit,
                                —take care:
—Your rival's speech has scored.
                              —Some crushing *tour de
force,*
—some master stroke,
                        —is needed now.
                                —The stage is yours.

KORYPHAIOS

Unless your strategy is shrewdly planned and your attack
    ferocious,
then your cause is lost. We'll laugh you out of court.

SOPHISTRY

                                        At last!
A few minutes more and I would have exploded from sheer
    impatience
to refute him and demolish his case.
                            Now then, I freely admit
that among men of learning I am—somewhat pejoratively—
    dubbed
the Sophistic, or Immoral, Logic. And why? Because I first
devised a Method for the Subversion of Established Social
    Beliefs
and the Undermining of Morality. Moreover, this little
    invention of mine,
this knack of taking what might appear to be the worse
    argument
and nonetheless winning my case, has, I might add, proved
    to be
an *extremely* lucrative source of income.
                            But observe, gentle-
    men,
how I refute his vaunted Education.

To Philosophy.

                      Now then, in your curriculum
hot baths are sternly prohibited. But what grounds can you possibly adduce
for this condemnation of hot baths?

PHILOSOPHY

                     What grounds can I adduce? Why, they're thoroughly vicious. They make a man
flabby and effeminate.

SOPHISTRY

You can stop right there, friend. I have you completely at my mercy.
Answer me this: which of the sons of Zeus was the most heroic?
Who suffered most? Performed the greatest labors?

PHILOSOPHY

                        In my opinion,
the greatest hero who ever lived was Herakles.

SOPHISTRY

                        Very well then.
But when we speak of the famous Baths of Herakles,* are
we speaking of hot baths or cold baths? Necessarily, sir, of
hot baths. Whence it clearly follows, by your own logic,
that Herakles was both flabby and effeminate.
                     Q.E.D.

PHILOSOPHY

               Q.E.D.! This is the rubbish I mean!
This is the logical claptrap so much in fashion with the young!
This is what fills the baths and empties the gymnasiums!

SOPHISTRY

Very well,
if you like, consider our national passion for politics and debating,

pastimes which you condemn and I approve. But surely, friend,

if politics were quite so vicious as you pretend, old Homer—*

our mentor on moral questions—would never have portrayed Nestor

and those other wise old men as politicians, would he? Surely
he would not.

Or take the question of education in oratory—
in my opinion desirable, in yours the reverse. As for Moderation and Decorum,

the very notions are absurd. In fact, two more preposterous or pernicious prejudices, I find it hard to imagine. For example,

can you cite me *one* instance of that profit which a man enjoys

by exercising moderation? Refute me if you can.

PHILOSOPHY

Why, instances abound.
Er . . . Peleus,* for example. His virtue won him a sword.

SOPHISTRY

A sword,
you say? What a charming little profit for the poor sucker!
Look at our Hyperbolos: nothing virtuous about *him*, god
knows, and yet, what with peddling lamps—plus a knack for
swindling—he piled up a huge profit. All cold cash. No
swords for him. No sir, Hyperbolos and swords just don't
mix.*

PHILOSOPHY

Furthermore,
Peleus' chastity earned him the goddess Thetis for his wife.

SOPHISTRY

> Precisely,
> and what did she do? Promptly ditched him for being cold,
> no passion for that all-night scrimmage between the sheets
> that lusty women love,
>> Bah, you're obsolete.

To Pheidippides.

> —Young man,
> I advise you to ponder this life of Virtue with scrupulous
>   care,
> all that it implies, and all the pleasures of which its daily
>   practice
> must inevitably deprive you. Specifically, I might mention
>   these:
> Sex. Gambling. Gluttony. Guzzling. Carousing. Etcet.
> And what on earth's the point of living, if you leach your
>   life
> of all its little joys?
>> Very well then, consider your natural needs.
> Suppose, as a scholar of Virtue, you commit some minor
>   peccadillo,
> a little adultery, say, or seduction, and suddenly find yourself
> caught in the act. What happens? You're ruined, you can't
>   defend yourself
> (since, of course, you haven't been taught). But follow me,
>   my boy,
> and obey your nature to the full; romp, play, and laugh
> without a scruple in the world. Then if caught *in flagrante,*
> you simply inform the poor cuckold that you're utterly
>   innocent
> and refer him to Zeus as your moral sanction. After all,
>   didn't he,
> a great and powerful god, succumb to the love of women?
> Then how in the world can you, a man, an ordinary mortal,
> be expected to surpass the greatest of gods in moral self-
>   control?
> Clearly, you can't be.

PHILOSOPHY

> And suppose your pupil, by taking your advice,

is promptly convicted of adultery and sentenced to be
    publicly reamed
up the rectum with a radish?* How, Sir, would you save him
    from *that?*

SOPHISTRY

Why, what's the disgrace in being reamed with a radish?

PHILOSOPHY

Sir, I can conceive of nothing fouler than being buggered
by a radish.

SOPHISTRY

                    And what would you have to say, my friend,
if I defeat you on this point too?

PHILOSOPHY

                        What *could* I say?
I could never speak again for shame.

SOPHISTRY

                        Very well then.
What sort of men are our lawyers?

PHILOSOPHY

Why, they're all Buggers.

SOPHISTRY

                Right!
What are our tragic poets then?

PHILOSOPHY

Why, they're Buggers too.

SOPHISTRY

                Right!
And what of our politicians, Sir?

PHILOSOPHY

Why, Buggers to a man.

SOPHISTRY

                    Right!
You see how stupidly you spoke?
And now look at our audience.
What about them?

PHILOSOPHY

                    I'm looking hard.

SOPHISTRY

And what do you see?

PHILOSOPHY

                    By heaven,
I see an enormous crowd of people,
and almost all of them Buggers.

Pointing to individuals in the audience.

See there? That man's a Bugger,
and that long-haired fop's a Bugger too.

SOPHISTRY

Then how do we stand, my friend?

PHILOSOPHY

I've been beaten by the Buggers.

Flinging his cloak to the audience.

O Buggers, catch my cloak
and welcome me among the Buggers!

*With a wild shriek Philosophy disappears into
his cage and is wheeled away into the Thinkery, just
as Sokrates comes out.*

SOKRATES

Well, what are your wishes? Will you take your son home,
or shall I instruct him in the Pettifogger's Art?

STREPSIADES

                    Teach him—
and flog him too. But remember: I want his tongue
honed down like a razor. Sharpen him on the left side
for piddling private suits, but grind him on the right
for Grand Occasions and Affairs of State.

SOKRATES

                    Sir,
you may depend upon me. I promise I'll send him home
a consummate little Sophist.

PHEIDIPPIDES

                    God, what a picture of misery—
a nasty, pasty-faced, consummate little stinker!

Exeunt Sokrates and Pheidippides into the Thinkery.

KORYPHAIOS

Very well, go in.

To Strepsiades.

            —You, Sir, shall live to regret your decision.

*Exit Strepsiades into his own house, as the
Chorus turns sharply and faces the audience.*

CHORUS

And now, Gentlemen of the Jury, a few brief words about
    the Prize
and the solid benefits you stand to gain by voting for *The
    Clouds*—
as you certainly should anyway.

                    First of all, when the season sets
for Spring and plowing time has come, we guarantee each
    judge's fields

the top priority in rain. Let others wait. Furthermore,
for his vineyards and orchards, we promise, perfect growing-
   weather:
no drought shall touch them, no flooding rains destroy.

                                        However,
if some presuming mortal dares dishonor our divinity,
let him savor his punishment:
                              His acres, hard, dry, and barren,
shall see no harvesting. No wine, no fruit, shall ripen for
   him.
And when the olives sprout, and the season's green festoons
the vines, *his* shall wither, battered by our ratatat of rain.
And when he's busy baking bricks, we'll snuff his kiln with
   water
and smash his tiles with cannonades of hail. If he, his friend,
or relatives should celebrate a wedding, we'll send a
   DELUGE down
and drown the wedding night in rain!
                              By god, we'll make him say
he'd rather be roasting in Egypt than have voted wrong
   today!

*Enter Strepsiades from his house, counting on
his fingers.*

STREPSIADES

Five days, four days, three days, two days, and then
that one day of the days of the month
I dread the most that makes me fart with fear—
the last day of the month, Duedate for debts,*
when every dun in town has solemnly sworn
to drag me into court and bankrupt me completely.
And when I plead with them to be more reasonable—
"But PLEASE, sir. Don't demand the whole sum now.
Take something on account. I'll pay you later."—
they snort they'll never see the day, curse me
for a filthy swindler and say they'll sue.
                                        Well,
let them. If Pheidippides has learned to talk,
I don't give a damn for them and their suits.
                                   Now then,
a little knock on the door and we'll have the answer.

He knocks on Sokrates' door and calls out.

Porter!
        Hey, porter!

Sokrates opens the door.

SOKRATES

Ah, Strepsiades. Salutations.

STREPSIADES

Same to you, Sokrates.

He hands Sokrates a bag of flour.

Here. A token of my esteem.
Call it an honorarium.* Professors always get honorariums.

Snatching back the bag.

But wait: has Pheidippides learned his rhetoric yet—
that swindling Rhetoric that performed for us just now?

SOKRATES

Taking the bag.

He has mastered it.

STREPSIADES

O great goddess Bamboozle!

SOKRATES

Now, sir, you can evade any legal action you wish to.

STREPSIADES

Really? Even if I borrowed the money before witnesses?

SOKRATES

Before ten thousand of them. The more the merrier.

STREPSIADES

In parody.

> Then let my loud falsetto peal
> with gladsome paeans plangent!*
> Mourn, O ye lenders of money,
> weep, O principals! Gnash your teeth,
> O ye interests compounded.
> For lo, within mine halls
> a son hath risen,
> a son with burnish'd tongue,
> yea, with double edges lambent!
> Hail, O hero of my halls,
> who delivered my domicile,
> who fractur'd mine enemies
> and drowned a father's dolor!
> Ho, fetch forth mine son
> forthwith! O my son,
> debouch from mine abode!*
> O heed thy father, prithee!

*Pheidippides, the very image of "modern youth,"
slouches contemptuously out of the Thinkery.*

SOKRATES

Behold the man!

STREPSIADES

O joy! My boy!

SOKRATES

Take him and go.

STREPSIADES

O my son! O! O!
O! O! O! O!
Oh, how gladly I behold thy pasty face,
that negative and disputatious look! And see there,
how there blossoms on his lips our national rejoinder,
"Huh? G'wan!" How perfectly he is the rogue,
but looks the victim through and through. And on his face
that utter pallor, ah, that true Athenian look!

—All right, Son, you ruined me so it's up to you
to save me.

PHEIDIPPIDES

What's eating *you*, Dad?

STREPSIADES

Your damn debts.
And the date. That's what. Your debts are due today.
Today's Dueday.*

PHEIDIPPIDES

Today's two days? Or two Duedays?
But how can one day be two days?

STREPSIADES

How should *I* know?
It just *is!*

Resuming more calmly, patiently explaining.

Today's Dueday, son. *This* is the day
when creditors are required by law to post their bond*
in court in order to obtain a summons against their debtors.
No bond, no summons.

PHEIDIPPIDES

Ergo, they will forfeit their bond.
By definition, one day cannot be two days.

STREPSIADES

It *can't* be?
But why not?

PHEIDIPPIDES

Because it's a logical impossibility, numskull.
If one day were two days, then *ipso facto* a woman
could be simultaneously a young girl and an old hag.
Which she can't be.

STREPSIADES

But it's the law!

PHEIDIPPIDES

In that case,
I suspect the law on debt has been profoundly misinterpreted.

STREPSIADES

Misinterpreted? But how?

PHEIDIPPIDES

Enigmatically.

Old Solon loved the people.

STREPSIADES

And what in god's name has that got to do with the Duedate?

PHEIDIPPIDES

Solon's sympathies lay with the debtor, not with the creditor.

STREPSIADES

And so?

PHEIDIPPIDES

And so, when Solon promulgated his law on debt,
he carefully specified *two* distinct Duedates
for debts, not *one*, as the current interpretation has it.
Prima facie, a summons *could* be issued on either day,
though in practice this was impossible, since the creditor's
bond could be paid only on the second Duedate.

STREPSIADES

But why did Solon

set two Duedates?

PHEIDIPPIDES

Read between the lines, moron.
Solon intended that the debtor should present himself in
court on the first date and declare himself absolved of his
debts on the grounds of the creditor's failure to issue a
summons. He won by default. *If,* however, the debtor failed·
to take advantage of the deliberate ambiguity of the law,
he had to account to his creditors in court the next day.
Not an attractive prospect.

STREPSIADES

But wait. If that's the law,
then how do you account for the glaring fact that the magistrates actually demand that the creditor's bond be paid on
the first day and not on the second?

PHEIDIPPIDES

Precisely because they
are magistrates.*
Ipso facto, their greed is magisterial and their gluttony
uncontrollable. And because they can't wait to get their
fingers in the pie, they have quietly connived among
themselves to set the Duedate back a day earlier. Their
procedure, of course, is utterly illegal.

STREPSIADES

Still perplexed.

Huh?

But suddenly illuminated.

Hey!

Haw, that's good!

Turning to the audience.

Well, numskulls, what are *you* gawking at?
Yes, *you* down there!
You dumb sheep with the pigeon faces!

Cat's-paws for cleverer men! Any sophist's
suckers!
      O shysterbait!
               Generation of dupes!
Poor twerps, poor silly saps!
               O Audience of Asses,
you were born to be taken!
               —And now, gentlemen, a song.
A little ditty of my own, dedicated to me and my son,
offering us warmest congratulations on our success.
                              Ready,
everybody?

Singing and dancing.

> *Oh, Strepsiades, Strepsiades,*
> *there's no one like Strepsiades!*
> *He went to school with Sokrates*
> *who taught him all his sophistries!*
> > *He's smarter than*
> > *Euripides,*
> > *for only he's,*
> > *yes, only he's*
> > *Pheidippides'*
> > *Old Man!*

    By god, if ever I heard a hit, that's it!

To Pheidippides.

Once you finish off my creditors' suits, the whole town
will go green with envy of Strepsiades.
                    And now, son,
I'm throwing a dinner in your honor. So let's go in.

Exeunt Strepsiades and Pheidippides into the house.
An instant later Pasias arrives, accompanied by
his Witness, with a summons against Strepsiades. A
notorious spendthrift, drunkard, and glutton, Pasias
is grotesquely fat. Essentially a good-natured
man, he has prepared himself for a difficult ordeal,
and comes equipped with a wine flask from which
he periodically fortifies himself.

PASIAS

Well,
what am I supposed to do? Throw my hard-earned money
down the drain?

*Something in his own words reminds him that
he needs a drink, a stiff one.*

Playboy Pasias, is it?
Nossiree.
Bah! Me and my great big heart! Soft-touch Pasias.
But I should have known. You've got to be a bastard.
Hard as nails.

He hardens himself with a drink.

If I'd sent him packing when he tried
to put the touch on me, I wouldn't be in this fix now.
What a mess!

To Witness.

I have to drag you around to stand witness,
and what's more, I'll make an enemy of Strepsiades for life.

He fortifies himself with still another drink.

Well, I'll sue him anyway.
Yessiree.
Athens expects it,
and I won't have it said that Pasias ever besmirched
the National Honor.*
Nossiree.

Shouting into the house.

—Strepsiades! I'm suing you!

STREPSIADES

Appearing at the door.

Somebody want me?

PASIAS

I do. Today's the Dueday.

STREPSIADES

To the audience.

Gentlemen, you're all witnesses: he distinctly mentioned *two* days.

To Pasias.

—What are you suing me for?

PASIAS

What *for?* Why, the money you borrowed from me to buy that horse.

STREPSIADES

Horse? *What* horse? Everybody knows I'm allergic to horses. Ask the audience.

PASIAS

By god, you swore you'd pay me! You swore it by the gods.

STREPSIADES

Well, by god, now I swear I won't. Anyway, that was before Pheidippides learned th
Science of Unanswerable Argument.

PASIAS

And *that's* why you won't pay me

STREPSIADES

Can you think of a better reason? I'm entitled to some retur
on his education, aren't I?

PASIAS

And you're prepared to perjure yourself
on an oath sworn by the gods?

STREPSIADES

By the gods?
What gods?

PASIAS

What gods?
Why, Zeus, Poseidon, and Hermes.

STREPSIADES

Damn right
I would. And what's more, I'd do it again. Gratis,
by god!
I *like* perjury.

PASIAS

Why, you barefaced swindler!
You damnable liar!

STREPSIADES

Prodding Pasias in the belly.

Boy, what blubber!
—You know,
that paunch of yours ought to make someone a mighty
dandy wineskin . . .

PASIAS

By god, that's the last straw!

STREPSIADES

Hmmmm. Yup,
five gallons, I'd guess offhand.

PASIAS

So help me Zeus!
So help me every god in heaven, you won't get away
with this!

STREPSIADES

You know, you and your silly gods tickle me.
Zeus is a joke to us Thinking Men.

PASIAS

By god, someday
you'll regret this.
Now then, for the last time,
will you pay me or won't you? Give me a straight answer
and I'll be off.

STREPSIADES

Don't you budge. I'll be right back
and bring you my final answer.

Strepsiades rushes into the house.

PASIAS

To his Witness.

I wonder what he's doing.
Do you think he'll pay me?

STREPSIADES

*Reappearing from the house; in his hands he
holds a large basket.*

Now where's that creditor of mine?

Holding up the basket in front of Pasias.

—All right, you, what's this?

PASIAS

That? A basket.

STREPSIADES

A basket?
And a stupid ignoramus like you has the nerve to come
around badgering me for money? By god, I wouldn't give a
cent to a man who can't even tell a basket from a baskette.

PASIAS

Then you won't pay me back?

STREPSIADES

Not if *I* know it.
Look here,
you Colossus of Lard, why don't you quietly melt away?
Beat it, Fatboy!

He threatens to beat him with his baskette.

PASIAS

I'm going. Yessiree. And by god,
if I don't post my bond with the magistrates right now,
my name's not Pasias.
Nossiree.

STREPSIADES

Tch tch. Poor Pasias.
You'll just lose your bond on top of all your other losses.
And, personally speaking, I wouldn't want to see you suffer
just because your grammar's bad.

Beating Pasias over the head with his baskette.

Remember?
Baskette!

*Exit Pasias at a run pursued by Strepsiades. An
instant later, hideous wails and shrieks are heard offstage, and these are followed by the pathetic
entrance of the notorious effeminate and gambler,
Amynias. He has just had an accident with his
chariot, and his entrance is a picture of misery: his*

*head is covered with blood, his clothes torn, and
his language, a delirious compound of tragic rhetoric
and a marked lisp, is almost unintelligible.*

AMYNIAS

Alackaday!

     Woe is me!

          Alas!   Alas!

STREPSIADES

               Gods in heaven,
what a caterwauling!
      —Look, who *are* you?
             The way you whine
you sound like some poor blubbering god from a tragedy
by Karkinos.*

AMYNIAS

     *Wouldst hear how I am hight? Know then:
a wretched wight in woe am I, Adversity
yclept.*

STREPSIADES

    Then hit the road, Buster.

AMYNIAS

             O Funest Doom!
O Darkling Destiny!
        How fell the fate by which I fall,
ah, Pallas!
      O all unhors'd! O human haplessness
I am!

STREPSIADES

    I get it. You're an actor, and you want me to guess
what part you're practicing.
           Hmm.
             Must be a female role.
But of course!
       You're Alkmene in the play by Xenokles,
and you're mourning your brother . . .

AMYNIAS

You're *such* a tease,
you naughty man.

Now then, be a dear, and ask Pheidippides
to pay me my money. You see, I'm in the most frightful
way. You simply can't *imagine!*

STREPSIADES

Money? What money?

AMYNIAS

Why, the money
Pheidippides borrowed.

STREPSIADES

Hmmm. You *are* in a frightful way.
You simply can't *imagine*.

AMYNIAS

But I *can*. You see, on my way,
I was thrown from my chariot. Literally *hurled* into the air.
It was *too* awful.

STREPSIADES

It fits. You must have hurt your head.
That would explain that gibberish about money.

AMYNIAS

What's gibberish
about wanting my money?

STREPSIADES

Obvious case of delirium.
Brain damage too, I suspect.

AMYNIAS

Brain damage?

STREPSIADES

Yup.
You'll probably be queer the rest of your life. That's how
I see it.

AMYNIAS

Pay me my money, or I'll sue you! That's how
I see it.

STREPSIADES

Is that so?
All right, let me ask you a question.
I'm curious to know which theory on rainfall you prefer.
Now then, in your considered opinion, is the phenomenon
of rain best explained as a precipitation of *totally* fresh
water, or is it merely a case of the same old rainwater in
continuous re-use, slowly condensed by the Clouds and then
precipitated once more as rain?

AMYNIAS

My *dear* fellow,
I really couldn't care less.

STREPSIADES

Couldn't care less, eh?
And a sophomore like you, completely ignorant of Science,
thinks he's got the right to go around pestering people
to pay him money?
Boy, some nerve!

AMYNIAS

Look here,
if you're temporarily short of cash, then let me have
the interest.

STREPSIADES

Interest? What the devil's interest?

AMYNIAS

Why, interest
is nothing more than the tendency of a cash principal
to reproduce itself by increments over a period of time.
Very gradually, day after day, month after month,
the interest accrues and the principal grows.

STREPSIADES

Dandy.
Then in your opinion there's more water in the ocean now
than last year? Is that right?

AMYNIAS

But, of course, it isn't.
Oceans *can't* grow, you silly man. It's against the Law
of Nature.

STREPSIADES

Then what about you, you unnatural bastard?
If the ocean, with all those rivers pouring into it,
doesn't grow, then who the hell are you to expect your
money to grow?
And now CLEAR OUT! Go peddle your
subpoenas somewhere else.

*Amynias stands firm and Strepsiades calls out
to his slave.*

—Bring me my horsewhip.

*The slave brings the whip and Strepsiades cracks
it threateningly at Amynias.*

AMYNIAS

Appealing in terror to the audience.

—Gentlemen,
you're my witnesses!

STREPSIADES

Still here, are you?

He flicks Amynias with the whip.

Giddeap!

Gallop, you gelding!
Gee!

*He flicks Amynias again with his whip. this time
in the rear.*

AMYNIAS

A hit! A hit!

A palpable hit!

STREPSIADES

Raising his phallus to the ready.

Git, dammit, or I'll sunder your rump
with my ram!

*With a wild whinny of fright, Amynias
rushes offstage.*

Going, are you?
A damned good thing.
And don't come back here nagging me about your money,
or I'll badger your bum!
You'll get the ride of your life!

*Strepsiades re-enters the house to resume his inter-
rupted dinner with Pheidippides.*

CHORUS

Individually.

—Such is wickedness,
—such is fatal fascina-

tion:
—this senile amateur of fraud,
—by greed
and guile obsessed,
—frantic to disown his debts
—(and,
—such his luck,
—apparently
—succeed-

ing).

 —BUT please take note:

      —soon,

        —perhaps today,

—this poor man's Sokrates must learn his lesson,

—*viz.*

  —CRIME DOES NOT PAY.

         —Dishonesty

comes home to roost.

     —It's Poetic Retribution!

—But *now*, poor fish!

     —he thinks he's sitting

         —pretty.

—Success at last!

     —For hasn't his Pheidippides

become

   —so voluble a speaker,

       —so specious

a sophist,

   —a shyster so vicious,

      —that he's

now

  —ABSOLUTELY INVINCIBLE?

        —So

he gloats.

   —But wait!

     —Take note:

       —the time will come—

Strepsiades howls in pain offstage.

 —in fact, it's coming now—

       —when poor Strepsiades

will wish to god

    —Pheidippides were

       —DUMB!

*With a bellow of pain and terror, Strepsiades
plunges out of his house, hotly pursued by Pheidippides with a murderous stick.*

STREPSIADES

OOOUUUCH!!!

    HALP!

      For god's sake, help me!

Appealing to the Audience.

                                                 Friends!
Fellow-countrymen! Aunts! Uncles! Fathers! Brothers!
To the rescue!
                    He's beating me!
                                    Help me!
                                                Ouuch!
O my poor head!
                    Ooh, my jaw!

To Pheidippides.

                                    —You great big bully,
Hit your own father, would you?

PHEIDIPPIDES

                                    Gladly, Daddy.

STREPSIADES

You hear that? The big brute *admits* it.

PHEIDIPPIDES

                                    Admit it? Hell,
I *proclaim* it.

STREPSIADES

            You cheap Cutthroat!
                            You father-beating Bastard!
You Turd!
            You . . . you . . . you—

PHEIDIPPIDES

                            Carry on. Don't you know
you're complimenting me?

STREPSIADES

                Why, you . . . you . . . you Palpable Per-
vert!
You Pederast!

PHEIDIPPIDES

> Roll me in roses, Daddy!

STREPSIADES

> You Bugger!
> Hit you own father, would you?

PHEIDIPPIDES

> Damn right I would.
> God knows, I had good justification.

STREPSIADES

> *Justification,* you say?
> Why, you Dunghill, what justification could there *ever* be
> for hitting your own father?

PHEIDIPPIDES

> Would a logical demonstration
> convince you?

STREPSIADES

> A logical demonstration? You mean to tell me
> you can *prove* a shocking thing like that?

PHEIDIPPIDES

> Elementary, really.
> What's more, you can choose the logic. Take your pick.
> Either one.

STREPSIADES

> Either *which?*

PHEIDIPPIDES

> Either *which?* Why,
> Socratic logic or pre-Socratic logic. Either logic.
> Take your pick.

STREPSIADES

        Take my pick, damn you? Look,
who do you think paid for your shyster education anyway?
And now you propose to convince *me* that there's nothing
wrong in whipping your own father?

PHEIDIPPIDES

              I not only propose it;
I propose to *prove* it. Irrefutably, in fact. Rebuttal
is utterly inconceivable.

STREPSIADES

          By god, *this* I want to hear!

CHORUS

    Old friend, WATCH OUT.
    Upon this bout
      may hang your own survival.

    What's more, unless
    I miss my guess,
      the odds are on your rival.

    That curling lip,
    that sneer's a tip,
      and you'd be wise to heed it.

    The tip? A trap.
    But, *verbum sap.*
      I wish you luck. *You*'ll need it.

KORYPHAIOS

To Strepsiades.

And now, Sir, I suggest you brief the Chorus. Begin at the

beginning and describe your little fracas exactly as it
happened.

STREPSIADES

      Yes'm.
The whole damn dirty squabble from start to finish.
                      As you know,
we both went in to celebrate. Well, Ladies, a custom's a
  custom,*
after all, and there's nothing like a little music, I always say,
to get a party off to a good start. So naturally I asked him
to get down his lyre and sing a song. For instance,
  Simonides'
*Shearin' o' the Ram.**
      Well, you know what the little stinker answered?
That singing at table was—Obsolete,
                      Old Hat,
                          Lowbrow,
                              Bullshit!
Strictly for grandmothers.

PHEIDIPPIDES

              You damn well got what you
deserved. Asking me to sing on an empty stomach! What is
this anyway? A banquet or a cricket-concert?

STREPSIADES

              You hear that?
              A cricket-concert!
His exact words.
        And then he started sneering at Simonides!
Called him—get this—Puny Pipsqueak Hack!
                    Was I *sore?*
Brother!
  Well, somehow I counted to ten, and then I asked
him to sing me some Aischylos.
              Please.
                And you know what he
  replied?

That he considered Aischylos "a poet of colossal stature:"—

> Yup,

"the most colossal, pretentious, pompous, spouting, bombastic bore in poetic history."*

> I was so damn mad I just about went

through the roof. But I gritted my teeth together, mustered up a sick smile and somehow managed to say, "All right, son, if that's how you feel, then sing me a passage from one of those highbrow modern plays you're so crazy about."

> So he recited—you can guess—

Euripides! One of those slimy tragedies* where, so help me, there's a brother who screws his own sister!

> Well, Ladies, *that* did it!
>
> I jumped up,

blind with rage, started cursing at him and calling him names, and he started screaming and cursing back and before I knew it, he hauled off and—*wham!*—he biffed me and bashed me and clipped me and poked me and choked me and—

PHEIDIPPIDES

> And, by god, you

had it coming! Knocking a genius like Euripides!

STREPSIADES

> Euripides!
> A GENIUS??
> That . . .

That . . . that . . . !

Pheidippides raises his stick threateningly.

> HALP! He's hitting me!

PHEIDIPPIDES

> You've got it

coming, Dad!

STREPSIADES

Got it coming, do I?

> Why, you ungrateful brat, I *raised* you!

When you were a baby I pampered you! I waited on you
hand and foot!
I understood your babytalk. You babbled GOO and I
obeyed. Why,
when you whimpered WAWA DADA, who brought your
water?
DADA did.
When you burbled BABA, who brought your Baby Biscuits?
DADA did.
And when you cried GOTTA GO KAKA DADA, who
saved his shitty darling?
Who rushed you to the door? Who held you while you did
it? Damn you,

>   DADA did!
>   And in return you choked me
>   and when I shat in terror,
>   would you give your Dad a hand,
>   would you help me to the door?
>   No, you left me there alone
>   to do it on the floor!
>
>   *Yes, to do it on the floor!*

CHORUS

>   YOUR ATTENTION, PLEASE!
>   Pheidippides
>   now makes his demonstration—
>
>   a proof which will,
>   I'm certain, thrill
>   the younger generation.
>
>   For if this lad
>   defeats his Dad,
>   there's not an older man
>
>   or father in
>   this town, whose skin
>   is worth a Tinker's Damn!

KORYPHAIOS

And now that Doughty Champion of Change, that Golden-
   Tongued Attorney
for Tomorrow, that Harbinger of Progress
                                        —PHEIDIPPIDES!

To Pheidippides.

                                        Remember, Sir,

we want the truth
                —or a reasonable facsimile.

PHEIDIPPIDES

                                    Gentlemen, Eloquence
is sweet, sweeter than I ever dreamed! This utter bliss of
speech! This rapture of articulation! But oh, the sheer Attic
honey of subverting the Established Moral Order!
                            And yet when I look back
on those benighted days of pre-Sokratic folly, upon the boy
I used to be, whose only hobby was horses, who could not
speak three words of Greek without a blunder, why . . .
                                words fail me
But *now,* now that Sokrates has made a fresh Pheidippides
of me, now that my daily diet is Philosophy, Profundity,
Subtlety, and Science, I propose to prove beyond the
shadow of a doubt the philosophical propriety of beating
my Father.

STREPSIADES

            For the love of Zeus,
go back to your damn horses! I'd rather be stuck with a
stable than be battered by a stick.

PHEIDIPPIDES

                            I ignore these childish interruption
and proceed with my demonstration.
                            Now then, aswer my question
did you lick me when I was a little boy?

STREPSIADES

Of course I licked you.
For your own damn good. Because I loved you.

PHEIDIPPIDES

Then *ipso facto*,
since you yourself admit that loving and lickings are
synonymous, it's only fair that I—for your own damn good,
you understand?—whip you in return.

In any case by what right do you whip me
but claim exemption for yourself?

What do you think I am? A slave?
Wasn't I born as free a man as you?*

Well?

STREPSIADES

But . . .

PHEIDIPPIDES

But what?
Spare the Rod and Spoil the Child?

Is that your argument?

If so,
then I can be sententious too. *Old Men Are Boys Writ Big*,
as the saying goes.

A fortiori then, old men logically deserve
to be beaten more, since at their age they have clearly less
excuse for the mischief that they do.

STREPSIADES

But it's unnatural! It's . . . *illegal!*
Honor your father and mother.

That's the law.

Everywhere.

PHEIDIPPIDES

The *law?*

And who made the law?

An ordinary man. A man like you or me.
A man who lobbied for his bill until he persuaded the
people to make it law.

By the same token, then, what prevents me now
from proposing new legislation granting sons the power to
inflict corporal punishment upon wayward fathers?

Nothing vindictive,
of course.

In fact, I would personally insist on adding a rider,
a Retroactive Amnesty for Fathers, waiving our right to
compensation for any whippings we received prior to the
passage of the new law. However, if you're still uncon-
vinced, look to Nature for a sanction. Observe the roosters,
for instance, and what do you see?

A society
whose pecking-order envisages a permanent state of open
warfare between fathers and sons. And how do roosters
differ from men, except for the trifling fact that human
society is based upon law and rooster society isn't?

STREPSIADES

Look, if you want to imitate the roosters,
why don't you go eat shit and sleep on a perch at night?

PHEIDIPPIDES

Why? Er . . .
because the analogy doesn't hold, that's why. If you don't
believe me, then go ask Sokrates.

STREPSIADES

Well, whatever your roosters happen to do
you'd better not lick me. It's your neck if you do.

PHEIDIPPIDES

My neck?

How so?

STREPSIADES

Because look: I lick you. All right, someday you'll
have a son and you can even the score with me by licking
the hell out of him. But if you lick me, then your son will
follow your precedent by licking you. If you have a son.

PHEIDIPPIDES

And if I don't have a son?
You've licked me, but where am I? I'm left holding the bag,
and you'll go to your grave laughing at me.

*There is a long tense silence as the full force of this
crushing argument takes its effect upon Strepsiades.*

STREPSIADES

What?
But how . . . ?
Hmm,
by god, you're right!

To the Audience.

—Speaking for the older generation,
gentlemen, I'm compelled to admit defeat. The kids have
proved their point: naughty fathers should be flogged.

PHEIDIPPIDES

Of course, I nearly forgot.
One final matter.

STREPSIADES

The funeral?

PHEIDIPPIDES

Far from it. In fact,
it may even soothe your feelings.

STREPSIADES

How to be licked and like it, eh?
Go on. I'm listening.

PHEIDIPPIDES

Well, now, Misery Loves Company, they
say. So I'll give you some company:
I'll horsewhip Mother.

STREPSIADES

You'll *WHAT???*
HORSEWHIP YOUR OWN MOTHER?
But this is worse! Ten
thousand times worse!

PHEIDIPPIDES

Is that so? And suppose I prove by Sokratic logic the utter
propriety of horsewhipping Mother?
What would you say to that?

STREPSIADES

What would I
say?
By god, if you prove *that*,
then for all I care, you heel,
you can take your stinking Logics
and your Thinkery as well
with Sokrates inside it
and damn well go to hell!

To the Chorus.

—You Clouds got me into this! Why in god's name
did I ever believe you?

KORYPHAIOS

The guilt is yours, Strepsiades,
yours and yours alone. The dishonesty you did
was your own choice, not ours.

STREPSIADES

But why didn't you warn me
instead of luring a poor old ignoramus into trouble?
Why did you encourage me?

KORYPHAIOS

Because this is what we are,
the insubstantial Clouds men build their hopes upon,*
shining tempters formed of air, symbols of desire;
and so we act, beckoning, alluring foolish men
through their dishonest dreams of gain to overwhelming
ruin. There, schooled by suffering, they learn at last
to fear the gods.

STREPSIADES

Well, I can't say much for your methods,
though I had it coming. I was wrong to cheat my creditors,
and I admit it.

To Pheidippides.

—All right, boy, what do you say?
Let's go and take revenge on Sokrates and Chairephon
for swindling us. Are you game?

PHEIDIPPIDES

What? Raise a finger
against my old Philosophy professor? Count me out.

STREPSIADES

Show a little respect for Zeus.

PHEIDIPPIDES

Zeus?
You old fogy,
are you so stupid you still believe there's such a thing
as Zeus?

STREPSIADES

Of course there's a Zeus.

PHEIDIPPIDES

Not any more
there isn't. Convection-Principle's in power now.
Zeus has been deported.

STREPSIADES

That's a lie! A lot of cheap
Convection-Principle propaganda circulated by those
windbags in the Thinkery!
I was brainwashed! Why, they told me
that the whole universe was a kind of potbellied stove

Pointing to the model in front of the Thinkery.

like that model there, an enormous cosmical barbecue,
and the gods were nothing but a lot of hot air and gas
swirling around in the flue. And I swallowed it,
hook, line, and sinker!

PHEIDIPPIDES

Rave to yourself, Madman.
I'm leaving.

Exit Pheidippides.

STREPSIADES

O Horse's Ass, Blithering Imbecile,
Brainless Booby, Bonehead that I was to ditch the gods
for Sokrates!

*He picks up Pheidippides' stick and savagely
smashes the potbellied model of the Universe in front
of the Thinkery. He then rushes to his own house
and falls on his knees before the statue of Hermes.*

—Great Hermes, I implore you!

Be gracious,
lord! Forego your anger and give me your compassion.
Pity a poor old codger who was hypnotized with hogwash,
drunk on drivel.

O Hermes, give me your advice,
tell me what to do.

Should I sue?

He puts his ear close to the god's mouth as though
listening to whispered advice.

What?

Ummm.

Good.

Got it.

DON'T SUE ...

Go on.

Yes?

BURN DOWN THE THINKERY ... SMOKE OUT
THE CHARLATANS ...
INCINERATE THE FAKES!

Aye aye, Sir!

Shouting to his slave.

—Xanthias! come here!

Quick, get me your ladder!

Bring me an axe!

Xanthias runs up with a ladder and an axe.

Now
scramble up there on the Thinkery and rip up the tiles
until the roof caves in.

Shoo, boy!

Xanthias sets his ladder against the Thinkery,
clambers up, and starts chopping at the tiles and
prying them up with his axe.

—Quick,
bring me a torch!

Another slave runs up with a blazing torch.

By god, I'll fix those fakes
for what they did to me or my name's not Strepsiades!
Let's see if they can fast-talk their way out of this.

*He bounds up the ladder to the roof, furiously
firing the rafters and beams with his torch, while
Xanthias pries at the tiles with the axe. The smoke
billows up in clouds and the whole roof begins to
glare luridly, while inside the Thinkery are
heard the first signs of alarm and confusion.*

FIRST STUDENT

From within.

FIRE!! FIRE!!
          HELP!

STREPSIADES

                    Scorch 'em, Torch!
Go get 'em!

*When Xanthias stops to stare at the holoccust,
Strepsiades tosses him the torch, snatches up the axe,
and starts slashing furiously at the rafters.*

FIRST STUDENT

*Rushing out of the Thinkery and peering up
to the roof.*

          —Sirrah, what dost?

STREPSIADES

                    Dust? That's chips,
Buster. I'm chopping logic with the rafters of your roof.

SECOND STUDENT

From within.

Who roasteth our rookery?

STREPSIADES

                    A man without a coat.

SECOND STUDENT

Rushing outside.

But we're burning alive!

STREPSIADES

Hell, I'm freezing to death!

FIRST STUDENT

But this is Arson! Deliberate Arson! We'll die!

STREPSIADES

Splendid. Exactly what I had in mind—

He narrowly misses his leg with the axe and then teeters dangerously on the roof.

oops!—

so long as I don't split my shins with this axe
or break my neck in the process.

Wheezing, hacking, and gagging, Sokrates scuttles out of the Thinkery, closely followed by an incredible procession of emaciated, ghostlike Students, all gibbering with terror. Finally, at the very rear, squawking and clucking like two frightened roosters, come Philosophy and Sophistry.

SOKRATES

You there, sirrah!
What is thy purpose upon my roof?

STREPSIADES

Ah, sir,
I walk upon the air and look down upon the sun
from a superior standpoint.

SOKRATES

Choking on the smoke and almost incoherent with rage.

Why, you—

agh!

I'm gagging . . .

argh

I . . .

grhuahg . . . CAN'T . . .

TALK! !

Arrggghhh. . . .

*As Sokrates collapses into a spasm of choked
coughing, Strepsiades and Xanthias come scrambling
down the ladder from the roof. Then Chairephon,
totally covered with soot and cinders and his
cloak smouldering, streaks from the
holocaust of the Thinkery.*

CHAIREPHON

Yiyi

HALP!
It's like an oven in the Thinkery! I'm burnt to a crisp.
I'm a cinder.

STREPSIADES

*Belaboring him with a stick as Xanthias
lashes Sokrates.*

Then why did you blaspheme the gods?
What made you spy upon the Moon in heaven?

KORYPHAIOS

Thrash them
beat them, flog them for their crimes, but most of all
because they dared outrage the gods of heaven!

*Strepsiades and his slaves thrash Sokrates and
his followers until the whole herd of thinkers,
followed by Philosophy and Sophistry, stampedes
madly toward the exit. Here they meet—and flatten—
Pasias and Amynias* returning to the Thinkery
armed with summonses and accompanied by
their witnesses. Exeunt omnes in a general rout.*

Behind them the Thinkery with an enormous crash
collapses into blazing ruin.

CHORUS

> Now ladies, let us leave
> and go our way.
> Our dances here are done,
> and so's our play.

Slowly and majestically, the Chorus files out.

Notes

page 17. *Strepsiades:* A name derived from στρέψις (turning twisting, wriggling). That is, Strepsiades is etymologically The Debtdodger and his name is played upon throughout the play.

17. *desert to the Spartans:* The annual invasions of Attika by the Spartans and their allies during the first few years of the Peloponnesian War meant that maltreated or discontented Athenian slaves could easily desert to the enemy, and the fear of desertion was common in Athens.

18. *ponytails:* Pheidippides wore his hair long and curling in the style affected by the younger knights.

20. *bumbailiff:* B. B. Rogers' solution, perhaps too English for American ears; but the pun is almost untranslatable. The Greek word here translated as bumbailiff is δήμαρχος, inserted as a surprise in place of the expected "bedbug" or "flea."

20. *Blueblood Megakles:* Megakles was a common male name of the Alkmaionid family, one of the oldest and most aristocratic in Athens. It is largely because of the prominence of Alkmaionid names in the play that Pheidippides has frequently—and not improbably—been regarded as a caricature of Alkibiades, also an Alkmaionid and notorious for his dissolute youth.

Strepsiades' marriage to an Alkmaionid wife is, of course, a *mésalliance* between a prosperous farmer and a daughter of the dissolute and luxurious city nobility. Presumably, such alliances were not uncommon in the late fifth century, and Aristophanes clearly intends to show the progress of corruption in Strepsiades, ruined by his playboy son and his luxurious wife.

21. *hippos:* "Horse." A common component in aristocratic names, since in early Athens the ownership of a horse automatically meant membership in the military cavalry or the social chivalry.

page 21. *Pheidonides:* The name means Parsimonious.

  21. *Pheidippides:* The compromise means Parsimonious Chevalier or The Scrimping Aristocrat.

  22. *horse-god oaths:* As Poseidon Hippios, Poseidon was the patron god of horsemen. Cf. *Knights* 551 ff.

  23. *Cosmical Oven:* The theory advanced in this passage is of uncertain provenience. In *Birds* 1001, Aristophanes attributes it to Meton, though the comedian Kratinos attributed it to Hippo in his *Panoptai,* and both Herakleitos and Parmenides held that the heavens were made of Fire. Here, however, it is probably best taken as a representative—and, for Aristophanes, representatively ridiculous—example of contemporary physical theory. Some of the Sophists may have held something like it; so far as we know, Sokrates did not.

  But the metaphor of the Cosmical Oven is central to the play, and for this reason Aristophanes has placed a visible model of it in front of the Thinkery (cf. 11. 1473-74). Moreover, unless I am mistaken, the metaphor is a surprisingly consistent one, whose every detail and principle would have been instantly understood by an Athenian—but not an American —audience. For the principle here is that of an ordinary, humdrum, home-made charcoal-burner's "kiln," used incongruously as a diagram of highfalutin' Socratic physics, and it is in the appreciation of the details that the humor of the finale lies. It is, according to Aristophanes, a kiln designed for very slow heat and very little air (i.e., a πνιγεύς); in shape it is like an inverted bowl (i.e., a δῖνος—cf. 1. 1473), bellied at the bottom and tapered at the top; set inside it are charcoals (i.e., ἄνθρακες—1. 97) and *above* the charcoals are the swirling heated gases and flames (i.e., αἰθέριος δῖνος—1. 380) under whose steady heat wood becomes charcoal. Translated into the physics of the Aristophanic Sokrates, the humble charcoal-burner's oven becomes the Universal Crucible, in which the gods are the lightning and the slow, downward-burning heat of the heavens, the forces which slowly carbonize the world and the creatures below; in which living is a form of burning and the dead are only ashes.

Against this background, with only minor modifications, Sokrates' student can demonstrate to Strepsiades the cosmical principles involved in the gnat's buzz and Sokrates can explain the thunder as elemental farting. And it is, of course, the same metaphor which informs the finale of the play where the Thinkery itself becomes an enormous blazing kiln. Sokrates chokes on the smoke (ἀποπνιγήσομαι—1. 1504), Chairephon is roasted alive (κατακανθήσομαι —1. 1505), while Strepsiades, like a blazing god, fires the roof *above* them.

Such, I believe, is Aristophanes' meaning. Because, however, charcoal kilns are unfamiliar nowadays, I have been compelled to make the Cosmical Oven an ordinary potbellied stove and to introduce a pseudoscientific equivalent for Δῖνος, i.e., Convection-Principle.

page 23. for a fee: The perennial gibe. The Sophists expected to be paid for the instruction they gave, an attitude which seemed mercenary to the wealthy Plato and which Platonists since have never tired of condemning. Doubtless many of the Sophists were mercenary and several were rich men, but the mere fact of accepting a salary for professional services rendered does not—except in aristocratic societies where cash payments are regarded as vulgarizing those who receive them—convict a man of intellectual dishonesty. But perhaps I am prejudiced. In any case, the sophistic movement made headway in Athens, not because the Sophists were greedy mountebanks in a gullible age, but because there was a rising class with a desperate need for new skills and techniques and for this class the existing education was worse than useless. If the New Education began by being *vocational*—offering precisely those legal and verbal skills which were so urgently required for the conduct of Athenian imperialism—it ended by being genuinely *revolutionary,* that is, by systematically questioning and overturning all the established beliefs of the old order. It could never have become this, however, had not the fact of payment *freed* the Sophists from the old order as much as it *bound* them to the new. Hence the hostility and open contempt of such conservatives as Aristophanes and Plato.

Sokrates, it is true, did *not* accept payment, and this is Sokrates' glory. But Sokrates' glory is not necessarily the Sophists' shame.

page 23. *The Technique of Winning Lawsuits:* Literally, "to overcome the truth by telling lies," i.e., the familiar accusation that the Sophists made "the worse cause appear the better." It was precisely this charge that was brought against Sokrates by his accusers later, and Aristophanes may be responsible for the suspicion. That some Sophists professionally claimed this ability is beyond dispute. Equally, however, the sophistic attack upon traditional beliefs must have seemed both perverse and illogical to staunch conservatives. Passionately held convictions tend, i.e., to defend themselves by their look of being self-evident: those who question them are *ipso facto* guilty of dishonesty or faulty reasoning. And this is especially true of an age when logic was in a state of comparative infancy. Plato, for instance, constantly attacks the Sophists for their devotion to specious logic (i.e., sophistry), and yet his own *Republic* contains dozens of logical fallacies and grotesque equivocations that even a schoolboy could detect. And presumably these are honest mistakes. But the Sophists normally receive no mercy.

25. *two kinds of Logic:* i.e., the so-called Just (or Major or Better) Logic and the Unjust (or Minor or Weaker) Logic, here rendered as Philosophy and Sophistry respectively.

The originator of the Doctrine of the Two Logics (or *Antilogoi*) was Protagoras of Abdera. If we are right in assuming that Protagoras' famous dictum ("Man is the measure of all things") means that the truth is subjective, then the same statement also implies that a proposition can be simultaneously both true and false. And it is a fact that Protagoras taught his students to argue *both* sides of a given statement with equal plausibility—presumably as an exercise in forensic virtuosity. The very willingness of Athenian courts to consider matter that would now be regarded as inadmissible supports the view that these exercises were practical in scope and not deliberate attempts to subvert justice. But for Aristophanes the *Antilogoi* are transparent sophistry, humbug on a huge scale, and he accordingly makes the debate between the two *Logoi* the climax of the comedy.

It is customary, of course, to translate Λόγος as "Logic" or "Argument," and this is the literal meaning of the word. But the issue here is larger, and to translate this way tends to obscure the fact that Aristophanes is talking, not about systems of formal logic, but about a whole system of Reason, discursive and nondiscursive alike. Λόγος also means Reason; but Reason includes several modes of discourse ranging from the work of the imagination to moral reason and strictly logical reason in the narrow sense. The so-called Just Argument, for instance, is not really an argument or a logical system at all; it is a personification of the kind of Reason spoken by a certain kind of society before logic, strict logic, existed: a Reason which expressed itself in education, in morals, in imagination, in the criteria of values and the justifications offered for those values. As opposed to the Unjust Argument, it represents the rational power of poetry—and the peculiar logic of poetic imagination—against the rational power of prose and formal logic (and for this very reason Aristophanes lets the Just Argument speak in splendid anapests while the Unjust Argument uses prosy iambics). In ethics, it represents the power of rational suasion—by means of models and parallels drawn from the great body of lyric and epic poetry—in contrast to a system of ethics, just as rational but rational in a different way, sanctioned by inferences drawn from Nature and animal existence (cf. Pheidippides' inferences from the life of the rooster, 11. 1427-29). In culture, it is the rational guidance of Custom (not Blind Custom), the corrective rightness of traditional experience as against the restless innovations and risky isolation from experience and history of the pure intellect. It is not what the modern world normally means by Reason, and certainly not what Protagoras meant, but it is, I think, what Aristophanes meant and what most Greeks would have understood him to mean. But for this very reason, because his *Logos* is not a logic but a prelogical discourse of the whole human reason, the Just Argument is helpless against his opponent. His case cannot be expressed logically, and yet it remains rational.

All this may seem like compounding old humbug with new, but it is the justification I make for translating Δίκαιος Λόγος as Philosophy and Ἄδικος Λόγος as Sophistry. Sophistry, of course, should be taken in the strict sense of the word, Philosophy in the loose and unprofessional sense (as in the catchphrase, "a philosophy of life").

page 26. *miscarriage:* Probably a conscious echo of Sokrates' claim to be a midwife of ideas.

29. *Spartan prisoners from Pylos:* Cf. Glossary, under *Pylos.* After their imprisonment, the Spartans must have been considerably emaciated.

29. *geological research:* Literally, "they are exploring the things under the earth." This was, in fact, one of the accusations brought against Sokrates by his accusers in 399 B.C. In substance the charge implies that scientific research is blasphemous, insofar as the very act of investigating Nature suggests that the inquirer has doubts about the received cosmology. In the *Apology*, Sokrates admits to having dabbled in scientific research in his earlier days; the later Sokrates, Plato implies, had quite outgrown such nonsense.

31. *And as patriotic as it is useful:* During the years preceding the Peloponnesian War, Athens sometimes confiscated the territory of rebellious subject cities. The land so confiscated was then divided by lot and portioned out among the poorer citizens of Athens. Such allotments, needless to say, were enormously popular—at least in Athens.

31. *a single lawcourt in session:* The Athenian love of litigation was notorious, and Aristophanes never misses a chance of hitting it. Cf. *Wasps.*

32. *Perikles squeezed it dry:* Cf. Glossary: EUBOIA.

page 35. *Bars of iron, like the Byzantines?*: Sokrates' statement that the gods are an expression coined by vulgar superstition causes Strepsiades to think of a less vulgar sort of coinage. And so he comes up with the Byzantines who, alone in the Greek world, used coins made of iron.

35. *the mystical couch*: Probably a very battered settee. The reader should perhaps be aware that the whole scene of Strepsiades' admission to the Thinkery and introduction to the Clouds is an elaborate "philosophical" initiation rite, probably paralleling initiation into one of the many Greek mysteries. Thus Sokrates' researches are *mysteries*; Sokrates powders Strepsiades as a *purification*; Strepsiades wears a *chaplet* and is forced to strip *naked* (like a candidate at the Eleusinian Mysteries) before entering the *cave* at the rear of the Thinkery (which reminds him of the cave of the oracular Trophonios, a Theban seer). After his entrance he must undergo an *ordeal* (whippings, bedbugs, etc.) before being vouchsafed rebirth as a *new man*.

35. *poor Athamas*: Cf. Glossary: ATHAMAS. Athamas attempted to kill his son Phrixos; when sentenced to be sacrificed for the attempt, he was saved by Herakles. The point here is that Strepsiades' mythology is inaccurate and his literary education has been neglected. But since no conceivable modern audience can be expected to know—or even to care—whether Athamas was killed or saved, I have deliberately intruded the two succeeding lines in the hope of making them seem Aristophanic and the situation a little clearer.

41. *That's why they write*: Presumably all the effusions which follow this are genuine examples of what happened when the Murky Muse inspired a dithyrambic soul.

52. *But I'm not a burglar*: According to the Scholiast, this line is explained by the customary Athenian procedure for searching a house in which stolen goods might have been hidden. The searcher was required to strip so that he could not, under pretense of carrying out his search, convey into the house of the accused the goods presumed to have

been stolen. Sokrates' reply in the following line is an intruded gloss of my own manufacture, designed to give the situation a possible point for a contemporary audience.

page 53. *ARISTOPHANES:* In the Greek text the speech which I have here assigned to Aristophanes is given to the Chorus in accordance with the normal convention of the *parabasis*. But if the Chorus in a normal *parabasis* speaks *on behalf of* the poet, the parabasis of *Clouds* is unique in having the Chorus speak, in the first person, *as* the poet himself. Doubtless in the original version of this play, the *parabasis* was spoken by the Chorus on the poet's behalf; but in the revision Aristophanes has laid aside the mask and speaks directly for himself. In the circumstances it seemed unnatural to give the Chorus the poet's lines, and I have therefore brought Aristophanes on stage to speak for himself in person.

54. *a stranger rescued the foundling:* Aristophanes had produced his comedy *The Banqueters* under the name of Kallistratos. His reason for so doing, he claims, was natural modesty and observation of Athens' neglect and mistreatment of her comic poets (cf. *Knights* 514-45); more likely, he was too young to enter the contest under his own name.

54. *Elektra in the play:* Cf. Glossary: ELEKTRA.

55. *dangling thong of leather:* The comic phallus. Despite the almost unanimous consensus of scholars that Aristophanic characters did *not* wear the phallus, and Aristophanes' explicit denial here, I am nonetheless convinced they did. My only argument is the text and the near impossibility of explaining the dramatic action of numerous scenes in the absence of the phallus. In *Clouds*, Strepsiades' little play on "finger-rhythm" (652 ff.) literally requires the phallus, as does his parting threat to Amynias (1299-1302). The masturbation-jingle in *Knights* (24 ff.) is unactable without it; the Wasps are stingless, etc., etc. Nor am I in the least deterred by Aristophanes' denial—the prize evidence of those who deny the phallus in Aristophanes—simply because it would be the height of ingenuousness, I

think, to take Aristophanes' word for it, especially here. *The Clouds* may very well be a daintier, wittier play than the comedies of Aristophanes' rivals, but the disclaimers here are slyly contradicted by the play: several scenes are pure slapstick, Strepsiades beats his opponents with a stick, etc.

page 56. *a dirty dance:* That is, the *kordax*. Cf. Glossary: KORDAX.

56. *my celebrated simile on the eels:* Cf. *Knights* 864-67.

57. *Paphlagon:* Cf. Glossary: PAPHLAGON.

57. *hard on the heels of the Levin rattled the steeds of Thunder?:* A quotation from Sophokles' (lost) *Teukros*.

57-58. *How the moon, in dudgeon, snuffed her flame amongst the rack, and the sun in sullenness withdrew:* An eclipse of the moon took place in October 425, and a solar eclipse in March 424, just before the election of Kleon as general.

59. *your month is a consequent chaos:* An allusion to the confusion created in the Hellenic calendar by the Athenian astronomer Meton. Instituted in 432 B.C. and then gradually adopted throughout Greece, the Metonic calendar changes made for initial difficulties. Because the reform was not uniformly adopted throughout Greece, the same festivals in different places would fall on different dates, etc.

60. *stripped Hyperbolos of his seat:* Hyperbolos (cf. Glossary) had been appointed Athenian delegate to the Amphictyonic Council of Delphoi in 424 B.C. The Council was a religious and juridical federation of Greek city-states whose primary concerns at this time would have been the war and infractions of such "international law" as existed at the time. Presumably, this Council would have been responsible for smoothing the way to general Greek adoption of the Metonic calendar. Exactly what happened to Hyperbolos is not known; the Chorus says that it "stripped him of his crown"—which may mean, as Rogers suggests, that the wind blew off the sacred chaplet which he wore in his official capacity. From the animosity of the Clouds, it can

be reasonably assumed that Hyperbolos had supported the Metonic reform.

page 62. *vulgarly called finger-rhythm:* δάκτυλος in Greek
means both "finger" and "dactylic meter."

62. *Raising his phallus to the ready:* Cf. note on pp.
142-43: *dangling thong of leather.*

63. *the female's a duchess:* An anachronistic pun of my
own invention; the Greeks had ducks but no dukes.
Literally, the Greek says "the male is a rooster
(ἀλέκτωρ), the female a roosterette (ἀλεκτρύαινα)."

63. *You've made basket masculine, when it's feminine:*
"Basket" is my own contribution. In the Greek, the
word is κάρδοπος, "a kneading-trough," whose -ος
termination is normally the sign of the masculine
gender, though κάρδοπος is in fact feminine. This
pun, of course, leads directly to discussion of
Kleonymos, another instance of a masculine ending
for an actual effeminate.

65. *Why, Amynia:* In the original, this whole passage
is based upon a play on the Greek vocative
(whereby the nominative *Amynias* becomes *Amynia*
—which has the -α termination of the feminine
nominative). Because English has no vocative, I
have recast the play here as a confusion between
singular and plural. For Amynias, cf. Glossary:
AMYNIAS.

70. *witchwomen from Thessaly:* Throughout antiquity,
Thessaly was famous for its red-headed witches.
Cf. Apuleius *Metamorphoses* I; Plato *Gorgias*
513 a.

72. *scorch out every word of the charges:* The charges
would have been written down on a wax tablet.

78. *Expended as required. No comment:* When asked
to account for the expenditure of several talents
(actually used to purchase the withdrawal of the
Spartans), Perikles answered only: "I spent them
as required."

79. *Even Hyperbolos:* Hyperbolos had evidently studied
under the Sophists for a fee of one talent—a large
sum.

80. *Philosophy and Sophistry:* Cf. note on pp. 138-40:
two kinds of Logic.

80. *from the neck up they are fighting-cocks:* Accord-

ing to a Scholiast, the Logics were garbed as fighting-cocks and brought out in cages. This statement
has rarely won the approval of scholars, who are
quick to point out that it is contradicted by the
references throughout the debate to hands, clothing,
and other parts of the *human* anatomy. If I am
right, the Logics wore rooster masks and a few
feathers with perhaps a great vivid bustle of tail
feathers; but from the neck down they were visibly
human. After their adoption by the Birds, Pisthe-
tairos and Euelpides appear garbed in this very way
(cf. *Birds*). Such a solution allows Aristophanes
to present the Logics as fighting-cocks or as wres-
tlers as his dramatic needs required, and the text
seems to me to support this.

page 82. *how Zeus escaped punishment after he imprisoned
his father?:* Zeus dethroned his father Kronos and
bound him in chains. The same argument is used
by Euthyphro (cf. Plato *Euthyphro*) to justify his
prosecution of his own father. But the argument
here is interesting because it shows clearly the
mythological rationale of the Old Education and
the way in which the New Education refuted it.
For the Old Education, mythology was a rational
corpus of heroic behavior and morality was taught
in mythological terms, quite despite the fact that
the morality of mythology was incompatible in
many instances with the operative moral values of
the fifth century. The greatest artists of the older
generation—Aischylos and Pindar—had in fact attempted to reconcile myth and moral behavior by
rewriting the offensive myths and expelling their
crudities or giving them new—and moral—interpre-
tations. The exponents of the New Education quite
naturally turned their characteristic invention—formal logic—against the Old Education by pointing
out the inconsistencies of its morality and mythology. The same purpose informs many of Euripides'
tragedies, and for this reason he incurred the suspicion and contempt of Athenian conservatives—
quite despite the fact that his own artistic intentions
were really very much like those of Aischylos, an
attempt to harmonize mythology and morality. But

because the morality was relatively new—or looked that way—and was supported by a logic which was destructive of the old morality, he was not understood by conservatives. Few artistic feuds seem, in fact, more futile than Aristophanes' with Euripides, since—apart from dramatic differences—the two men basically believed the same things.

page 84. *Telephos:* Cf. Glossary: TELEPHOS.

84. *Pandaletos' loaf:* Cf. Glossary: PANDALETOS.

86. *the Old Education:* Readers interested in knowing more about the conflict between different views of education in fifth-century Athens and the rationale of the Old Education should consult the relevant chapters of Werner Jaeger's *Paideia*. Suffice it to say here that it was basically a curriculum comprising two major fields called respectively Music and Gymnastic. By Music was meant the education of the inward man; the schooling not merely of the mind, but of the emotions, the "soul," the feelings and the thoughts in their rational ensemble. The basic instrument of this inward education was poetry joined to music, a blend in which poetry taught by means of example and emulation and was sustained by music which was believed to inculcate the moral virtues. Gymnastic was, of course, vigorous and disciplined athletics. The intended product of this theory of education was a disciplined reason in a disciplined body, an outward grace which expressed the grace and harmony within, the whole person embodying the classical virtues: self-control, decorum, respect for others, piety toward the gods, moderation in all things, dignity and courage. It was, in short, far more what we would call moral education, education in "character," than intellectual training. It was also, for obvious reasons, the education of a restricted and exclusive class. It taught no skills, prepared for no career, and was obviously impractical for Athenian society of the late fifth century. For these reasons, it has always appealed to the exponents of "education of character," British public schools and their American imitators. Aristophanes put his whole heart into its exposition here, and I have done my

best to overcome my own repugnance, though probably unsuccessfully.

It would, of course, have been a pleasure to modernize the debate and present it in topical terms as a struggle between the views of education represented—less than ideally, of course—by American universities and that preposterous pretence of education perpetrated by the professional "educationists" in the secondary schools of America. But this is a suggestion which might be adopted by a producer in search of a topical Aristophanes; for a translation, it is out of the question.

page 87. *A Voice from Afar* or *Hail, O Pallas, Destroyer!*: According to the Scholiast, the second of these hymns is ascribed to Lamprokles of Athens; the first to Kydeides of Hermione.

87. *their conduct was manly:* The point is precisely the manliness. The fashionable homosexuality of the Athenian upper classes was essentially borrowed from Sparta, where homosexuality was not only tolerated but even encouraged as a military virtue (because "lovers" would fight well for each other). Hence the contempt with which Philosophy regards the effeminate homosexuals of the Athenian New Education. Only among the Athenian lower classes was homosexuality viewed with contempt. The modern image of an Athens populated exclusively by happy philosophical pederasts is largely due to the fact that the surviving literature is a leisure-class production; poor men were very rarely Platonists.

92. *Baths of Herakles:* Greeks normally named hot baths everywhere the Baths of Herakles. Another example of specious logic against which Philosophy is helpless.

93. *old Homer:* This argument must have hurt. Of all the poets, Homer was regarded by the Old Education as the greatest, the Bible of true belief. And now, like the devil, Sophistry quotes scripture.

93. *Peleus:* Cf. Glossary: PELEUS.

93. *Hyperbolos and swords just don't mix:* Because Hyperbolos presumably attempted to avoid military service.

page 95. *reamed up the rectum with a radish?:* The poetic
punishment meted out to adulterers in Athens.

98. *Duedate for debts:* Strepsiades does not actually
say this. What he says is that the day he fears is
"the-Old-and-The-New." By this he means the effec-
tive last day of the lunar month, the day on which
both the last of the waning Old Moon and the first
of the waxing New Moon could be seen. The-Old-
and-The-New, in short, was the normal name given
to the last day of the month, the day on which
debts were payable. And this nomenclature con-
tinued to be used even when the calendar was no
longer lunar. The term is, to modern ears, grotesquely unfamiliar, but it is also crucial to an
understanding of the action, and for this reason I
have had considerable misgivings about altering it.
But upon reflection it seemed to me that "Duedate"
might possibly do, and I have so rendered it. But
see the note on this page: *Today's Dueday.*

99. *Call it an honorarium:* Aristophanes, that is, hints
that Sokrates was not above receiving "tokens of
esteem" from his disciples. This may be pure satiri-
cal malice, but then again it may not be. Sokrates'
students were mostly rich aristocrats; he himself was
poor. And in the circles which Plato frequented,
a distinction was probably drawn between a payment and a "gratuity"—the common sophistry of
"good society." But this is guesswork.

100. *with gladsome paeans plangent!:* An echo, according to the Scholiast, from the *Satyrs* of Phrynichos
—or Euripides' *Peleus.* Probably the latter.

100. *debouch from mine abode!:* A very slight modifica-
tion of Euripides' *Hekabe* 173 ff.

101. *Today's Dueday:* Cf. note above: *Duedate for
debts.* For a more literal rendering of Pheidippides'
sophistic analysis of the-Old-New-Day in the following lines, readers should consult any prose translation of the play. I have preferred to use the
"Dueday—two day" pun because it made the equiv-
ocation instantly visible as glib hocus pocus, though
it also meant a necessary change—a slight one—
in the interpretation of Solon's legislation which
Pheidippides offers. But I suppose most readers of

the *Clouds* to be more interested in a comedy than in the details of Athenian debt legislation.

page 101. *to post their bond:* Before commencing a legal action against a defaulting debtor, a creditor had to post with the prytanies, as caution money to defray court expenses, the sum of 10 per cent of the amount of the debt.

103. *Precisely because they are magistrates:* A deliberate distortion of the literal meaning of the Greek. The text actually says: "They act like Foretasters; in order to devour the meal as quickly as possible, they have the deposits paid a day in advance." The Foretasters seem to have been officials responsible for sampling the dishes to be served at a public feast the following day.

105. *the National Honor:* The National Honor (and, one might add, the public interest) of Athens required that every citizen be as litigious as possible.

110. *tragedy by Karkinos:* Karkinos was a frigid, fourth-rate tragedian with an apparent penchant for introducing querulous beggar-gods in his plays. Most of the fustian which follows is presumably the work of Karkinos or his son Xenokles. Talent did not run in the family.

119. *a custom's a custom:* The festive custom of *paroinia*, according to Rogers, an old convivial tradition of singing at table.

119. *Shearin' o' the Ram:* Krios (which also means "Ram") was a wrestler, probably the victim of an overwhelming defeat in a wrestling match, and hence the "Shorn Ram." Simonides' poetry was very highly regarded by the older generation.

120. *bombastic bore in poetic history:* The charge was common in antiquity. In an age of discursive prose and colloquial poetry, the gorgeousness of Aischylos and his extravagant metaphorical bravura made him look like a drunken lord of language. For Aristophanes, of course, Aischylos is the Model Poet who "makes men better citizens" as opposed to the Arch-Corrupter, Euripides Cf. *Frogs.*

120. *One of those slimy tragedies:* A reference to Euripides' (lost) *Aiolos.*

page 123. *Wasn't I born as free a man as you?:* A parody of Euripides' *Alkestis* 691.

127. *the insubstantial Clouds men build their hopes upon:* This line and most of the two which follow it are Arrowsmith, not Aristophanes. I have intruded them in order to give just a little more resonance to the meaning of the Clouds. For although English has idioms in plenty which more or less parallel the Greek—to "have one's head in the Clouds," "to build on the clouds," "castles in the clouds," etc.—a little further rounding out seemed necessary. The Clouds are the patrons of visionaries and woolgatherers the world over; here they are cloudy deceivers, the shining hopes that deceive Strepsiades.

132. *Pasias and Amynias:* The Greek plays, of course, have come down to us without footnotes or stage directions other than what the Scholiasts tell us. And I admit that there is no textual justification for bringing back Pasias and Amynias here, nor is it suggested by any Scholiast. They are here because Pasias threatened to pay his bond and return with a summons, and because I think Aristophanes would have liked them to be foiled again, even at Strepsiades' moment of truth.

Glossary

AISCHYLOS, AESCHYLUS: The great Athenian tragedian (525-456 B.C.).

AKADEME, ACADEMY: Originally a precinct sacred to the hero Akademos and afterward used as a gymnasium and recreation area. The general Kimon planted it with groves of olives and plane trees. Only in the fourth century, after becoming the haunt of the philosopher Plato and his followers, did the once athletic Academy become academic in the modern sense of the word.

AKROPOLIS, ACROPOLIS: The citadel of Athens.

ALKIBIADES: An Athenian politician (*ca.* 450-404) of great ability and brilliance. Of aristocratic Alkmaionid descent, he was related to Perikles and was, for some time, a devoted disciple of Sokrates. Distinguished by wealth, birth, and spectacular personal beauty, he spent his youth in lavish display and debauchery (Pheidippides in *The Clouds* has been thought to be a caricature of Alkibiades). After the death of Kleon in 422, Alkibiades became chief of the belligerent anti-Spartan party in Athens in opposition to the more conservative Nikias and was one of the primary advocates of the disastrous Sicilian expedition.

AMYNIAS: Son of Pronapes and one of Strepsiades' creditors in *The Clouds*. He was not, however, a professional moneylender but a notorious effeminate and wastrel, probably addicted to gambling.

ANTIMACHOS: A homosexual on a prodigious scale.

APOLLO: God of prophecy, music, healing, and light; his two chief shrines were at Delphoi (q.v.) and the island of Delos (q.v.).

ARTEMIS: Goddess of the hunt and the moon, sister of Apollo (q.v.).

ATHAMAS: King of Orchomenos and the legendary subject of a (lost) play by Sophokles. Having attempted to murder his son Phrixos (q.v.), Athamas was sentenced to be sacrificed. He was crowned with a sacrificial wreath and dragged before the altar, but just before being dispatched, was saved by the sudden intervention of Herakles.

ATHENA, ATHENE: Goddess of wisdom and war and patroness of Athens. On her breast she wore the aegis, a goatskin plated with scales and a Gorgon's head in the center.

BACCHOS: See DIONYSOS.

BYZANTION: A city on the Bosporos and a subject-city of the Athenian Empire. Its siege by the Athenians under Kimon in 469 was celebrated.

CHAIREPHON: A pupil and disciple of Sokrates; his scrawniness and emaciated pallor are constantly ridiculed by Aristophanes.

DELOS: Small Aegean island sacred to Apollo.

DELPHOI, DELPHI: A town in Phokis, celebrated for its great temple and oracle of Apollo.

DEMETER: The Earth-Mother; goddess of grain, agriculture, and the harvest, worshipped in her shrine at Eleusis in Attika.

DIONYSOS: God of vineyards, wine, and dramatic poetry; also called Bacchos, Evios, Bromios, etc.

ELEKTRA: Daughter of Agamemnon and Klytaimnestra; with her brother Orestes she murdered her mother for having killed her father. In the *parabasis* of *The Clouds*, Aristophanes alludes to the famous scene in Aischylos' *Choephoroe*, when Elektra recognized that her brother Orestes had returned to Argos from the lock of hair left on Agamemnon's tomb.

EPHESOS: A city in Asia Minor (Ionia), site of a famous temple of Artemis.

EUBOIA: A large and fertile island northeast of Attica. In 457 Perikles planted an Athenian colony on the island and otherwise exploited it. As a result the island revolted in 445 and had to be resubjugated. This time, however, Perikles' treatment of the island was so severe that it was commonly said (at least by his enemies) that he had "stretched Euboia on the rack of torture."

EUPOLIS: An Athenian poet of the Old Comedy and a rival of Aristophanes. Eupolis claimed that Aristophanes had imitated him in *The Knights*, and Aristophanes countered by charging that Eupolis' *Marikas* was a plagiarism of his own *The Knights*.

EURIPIDES· Athenian tragedian (480-406 B.C.) whose character and plays were constantly ridiculed by Aristophanes.

Euripides' mother may have been (though this is uncertain) a marketwoman who sold chervil, and Aristophanes never tires of twitting the tragedian about his mother's vegetables.

HERAKLES: Hero and demigod, son of Zeus and Alkmene; renowned for his great labors, his prodigious strength, and his gluttonous appetite.

HERMES: God of messengers and thieves; in Athens in every doorway stood a statue of Hermes (i.e., a herm, usually a pillar surmounted by a bust of the god), protector of the door and guardian against thieves—presumably because it takes a thief to keep another thief away.

HIERONYMOS: A dithyrambic poet and tragedian, notorious for his extraordinary shagginess, bestial appearance, and pederasty.

HIPPOKRATES: Athenian general and nephew of Perikles; his three sons, it seems, were all distinguished for their stupidity and were popularly nicknamed "The Pigs."

HYPERBOLOS: An Athenian demagogue, successor to Kleon on the latter's death in 422. Of servile origins, he seems to have been a peddler of lamps and then to have studied with the Sophists in order to advance himself politically. (At least these are the charges made against him by Aristophanes.) He was later ostracized and finally murdered by the oligarchical leaders in Samos.

KARKINOS: An Athenian tragic poet whose poetry and three sons are all ridiculed by Aristophanes. Karkinos' name means "Crab."

KEKROPS, CECROPS: Legendary first king of Attika and reputed founder of Athens. Hence "country of Kekrops" is equivalent to "Athens," and "son of Kekrops" to "Athenian." He is usually represented as twi-form, i.e., with the head and upper trunk of a man, but serpent-shaped below (symbolizing his earthborn origin).

KIKYNNA: An Athenian deme of the tribe of Akamantis.

KLEON: Son of Kleainetos; the most notorious and powerful of all Athenian demagogues. After the death of Perikles in 429 B.C., Kleon became, until his own death in 422, the leader of the radical democracy and the anti-Spartan extremists in Athens. An impressive speaker and a thoroughly unscrupulous and venal politician, he was bitterly loathed and attacked by Aristophanes. In 424 B.C., thanks to his coup in capturing the Spartan hoplites at Sphakteria, he reached the height of his power; so unchallengeable was his position that he was able to persuade the Athenians not to accept the handsome terms offered by Sparta in an attempt to recover her imprisoned hoplites. Filled with confidence in his military ability and tempted by the hope of further glory, Kleon took command of an Athenian army in Thrace, where, in 422, he was defeated and killed by the Spartan forces under Brasidas.

In Aristophanes' *The Knights,* Kleon is only slightly masked under the name of Paphlagon (q.v.).

KLEONYMOS: A corpulent glutton and part-time informer; Aristophanes' commonest butt for cowardice (i.e., throwing one's shield away).

KORDAX: A salacious dance commonly used in Athenian Old Comedy.

KRONOS: Father of Zeus, Hera, and Poseidon. Deprived of his rule by Zeus. Synonymous with "old fogy."

KYNTHOS: A mountain on the island of Delos, sacred to Apollo.

LEOGORAS: A wealthy Athenian gourmet, addicted to horse raising (or possibly to pheasant-breeding). Father of the orator Andokides.

LYDIA: A district of Asia Minor; under its greatest king, Kroisos (Croesus), it included almost all of Asia Minor from the river Halys to the Ionian coast. Its wealth and effeminacy were proverbial among Greeks.

MAENADS: The frenzied female worshippers (Bacchantes) of Dionysos (q.v.).

MAIOTIS: An inland sea (the modern Sea of Azov), northern arm of the Black Sea.

MARATHON: The famous battle (490 B.C.) in which the Athenian forces under Miltiades crushingly defeated the first Persian invasion of Hellas.

MEGAKLES: A name belonging to the Alkmaionid family, one of the proudest and most distinguished families of Athens.

MEMNON: Famous hero, son of Tithonos and Eos (Dawn); killed in the Trojan War at the hands of Achilleus.

MIMAS: A mountain on the coast of Ionia.

NESTOR: King of Pylos and a hero of the Trojan War, famous for his wisdom and eloquence.

OLYMPOS: Mountain (app. 9700 feet, alt.) in Thessaly, covered at the summit with perpetual snow and reputed by the Greeks to be the abode of the gods.

PALLAS: The goddess Athena (Pallas Athene).

PANATHENAIA: The great Athenian festival in honor of Athena.

PANDALETOS: A professional informer.

PAPHLAGON: Aristophanes' (and presumably Athens') nick-name for the demagogue Kleon (q.v.). The name is intended to suggest: (1) that Kleon came of slavish and foreign stock—i.e., was not an Athenian but a Paphla-gonian—and (2) the sheer volume and violence of Kleon's rhetorical assaults (from Greek *paphlazein*, to froth, bluster, storm).

PARNASSOS: A high mountain to the north of Delphoi (q.v.); one of the chief haunts of Apollo and the Muses, but fre-quented also by Dionysos.

PARNES: A mountain in the northeast of Attika, forming part of the boundary between Attika and Boiotia. Near its foot was situated the deme of Acharnai.

PASIAS: One of Strepsiades' creditors; evidently a grotesquely fat man and probably a drunkard to boot.

PELEUS: Hero of mythology, husband of Thetis and father of Achilleus. According to legend, Astydamia, wife of Akastos, fell in love with Peleus but was rejected by him. Angered, she denounced him to her husband for having attempted to seduce her. Akastos thereupon in-vited Peleus to a hunting expedition on Mt. Pelion, stripped him of his weapons, and left him to be torn to pieces by the wild animals. When Peleus was almost on the point of death, however, the god Hermes brought him a sword.

PERIKLES: Greatest of Athenian statesmen of the fifth cen-tury, and from 461 B.C. until his death in 429, the almost unchallenged leader of the radical Athenian democracy. Of one of Athens' most aristocratic families (the Alkmai-onids), he was nonetheless the politician most responsible for the creation of the extreme democracy of the late fifth century. To Aristophanes' critical and conservative eyes, it was Perikles who was responsible for the corruption of Athens, and Aristophanes never tires of contrasting the Athens of the Persian War period with the Athens of Perikles—corrupt, effete, cruelly imperialistic, avaricious, at the mercy of Sophists, clever orators, and impostors, cursed with a system (e.g., the law courts) which practi-cally guaranteed further excesses and injustices. Worst of all in Aristophanes' eyes was Perikles' belligerent war policies (e.g., the famous Megarian Decree of 432) and the fact that, after 429, Athens was left to the mercies of men like Kleon and Hyperbolos who lacked Perikles' restraint and political genius. Like almost all the comic dramatists, Aristophanes was a conservative (*not* an oligarch), and although he distinguishes clearly between Perikles and his corrupt successors, he nonetheless holds Perikles responsible for creating the political system in which men like Kleon could thrive.

PHOIBOS: Apollo (q.v.).

PHRIXOS: Son of Athamas (q.v.); on the point of being sacrificed to Zeus, he was rescued by his mother Nephele.

PHRYNICHOS: The famous early Athenian tragedian.

PHRYNIS: Of Mytilene, a famous citharist and musician of the fifth century; his innovations shocked and angered contemporary conservatives.

POSEIDON: Brother of Zeus and god of the sea. As god of the sea, he girdles the earth and has it in his power, as Poseidon the Earthshaker, to cause earthquakes. In still another manifestation, he is Poseidon Hippios, patron god of horses and horsemen.

PRODIKOS: Of Keos, the famous Sophist and friend of Sokrates.

PYLOS: Town of the southwestern coast of Messina whose siege and capture, along with the neighboring island of Sphakteria in 425-24, became a *cause célèbre* of the Peloponnesian War and the major source of Kleon's prestige and power in Athens. As a result of their defeat at Pylos and the capture of their hoplites, the Spartans were forced to sue for peace; every overture, however, was met by the determined refusal of Kleon, eager for the war to continue.

SARPEDON: Legendary hero, son of Zeus and Europa; killed by Patroklos during the Trojan War.

SIMON: A swindler, the details of whose peculations are unknown.

SIMONIDES: Of Keos, the great sixth-century lyric poet.

SOKRATES: (*Ca.* 469-399 B.C.) The great Athenian philosopher and teacher of Plato. In appearance he was almost grotesquely ugly; with his bulging eyes, fat lips, and a round paunch, he looked like nothing so much as a Satyr or Silenos. This, combined with his practice of strolling about the marketplace and accosting citizens with questions about truth, justice, beauty, etc., made him an apt target

for ridicule, all the more since it is doubtful whether the
majority of Athenians could, in fact, distinguish between
Sokrates and the average Sophist. That this is the case can
be inferred from *The Clouds* and Aristophanes' extremely
sophistic presentation of Sokrates.

SOLON: Famous Athenian legislator (*ca.* 638-588 B.C.), whose
achievement it was to have ended debt-slavery in Athens.

SOPHOKLES: The Athenian tragedian (495-404 B.C.).

TELEPHOS: Legendary king of Mysia and the subject of tragedies by Aischylos, Sophokles, and Euripides. Wounded
by Achilleus while defending his country, Telephos was
informed by an oracle that only the weapons which had
given him his wound would cure him. Thereupon, disguised as a beggar, he made his way to Argos where, with
the connivance of Klytaimnestra, he covertly took the
young Orestes hostage. When the gathered Greeks were
condemning Telephos for his hostility to their cause, the
disguised hero made a speech in his own defense, but
with such warmth and eloquence that the Greeks recognized him. When Achilleus demanded his death, Telephos
threatened to kill the infant Orestes. Finally, Achilleus
relented and agreed to give Telephos the weapon which
had wounded him and which would cure him.

THALES: Of Miletos (*ca.* 636-546 B.C.), one of the Seven
Sages of antiquity; renowned for his scientific genius and
for having predicted an eclipse of the sun.

THEOROS: Flatterer, perjurer, sycophant of Kleon.

THESSALY: A large district in northern Greece, renowned
throughout antiquity for its abundant supply of witches.

THETIS: The sea nymph, mother of Achilleus by Peleus
(q.v.). Courted against her wishes by Peleus, she changed
herself successively into a bird, a tree, and a tigress. But
Peleus, acting on the instructions of the centaur Cheiron,
countered by holding her fast until she assumed human
form and consented to marry him.

TLEPOLEMOS: Hero and son of Herakles, the subject of a
tragedy by the dramatist Xenokles, one of the sons of
Karkinos (q.v.). In the play one of the characters de-
scribes how his brother was killed by Tlepolemos.

TROPHONIOS: King of Orchomenos, worshipped as a hero after
his death. His oracle in a cave in Boiotia was celebrated
throughout Hellas, and those who consulted him made it
their practice to take honeycakes with which to appease

the snakes who frequented the cavern.

TYPHO, TYPHON: A fire-breathing giant, frequently represented as a hurricane.

XANTHIAS: A common servile name.

XENOKLES: An Athenian tragedian, son of Karkinos (q.v.).

XENOPHANTES: Father of Hieronymos (q.v.).

ZEUS: Chief god of the Olympian pantheon; son of Kronos, brother of Poseidon and father of Athena. As the supreme ruler of the world, he is armed with thunder and lightning and creates storms and tempests.

MENTOR Books of Special Interest

☐ **THE CREATIVE PROCESS, edited, with an Introduction, by Brewster Ghiselin.** Some of the greatest minds reveal how they begin and complete creative work in art, literature, science, and other fields.   (#MJ1729—$1.95)

☐ **THE ANCIENT MYTHS by Norma Lorre Goodrich.** A vivid retelling of the great myths of Greece, Egypt, India, Persia, Crete, Sumer, and Rome.   (#ME1714—$1.75)

☐ **THE GREEK EXPERIENCE by C. M. Bowra.** An extraordinary study of Greek culture, its achievements and philosophy. With 48 pages of photos.   (#ME1718—$1.75)*

☐ **THE GREEK PHILOSOPHERS edited by Rex Warner.** Basic writings of philosophers from Thales to Plotinus, revealing the roots of Western philosophy in ancient Greece.
                    (#MJ1716—$1.95)

☐ **GREAT DIALOGUES OF PLATO, translated by W. H. D. Rouse.** A new translation into direct, forceful English of "The Republic" and other dialogues of the great philosopher of ancient Greece.   (#ME1803—$2.95)

* Not available in Canada

Buy them at your local

bookstore or use coupon

on next page for ordering.

The MENTOR Philosophers

A distinguished series presenting in historical order the basic writings of the outstanding philosophers of the Western world —from the Middle Ages to the present time.

☐ **THE AGE OF BELIEF: The Medieval Philosophers edited by Anne Fremantle.** Basic writings of the most important philosophers from the 5th to the 15th century, including St. Augustine, Boethius, Abelard, St. Bernard, St. Thomas Aquinas, Duns Scotus, William of Ockam and others.
(#MJ1837—$1.95)

☐ **THE AGE OF REASON: The 17th Century Philosophers selected and edited by Stuart Hampshire.** Selections from the basic writings of Descartes, Leibniz, Spinoza and other great philosophers of "the century of Genius," when science began to influence philosophical thought. With penetrating Introduction and interpretive Commentary. (#ME1591—$1.75)

☐ **THE AGE OF ENLIGHTENMENT: The 18th Century Philosophers, selected and edited by Isaiah Berlin.** Basic writings of Berkeley, Locke, Voltaire, Reid, Hume and other brilliant philosophers of the rational and humanistic age which believed that science's achievements could be translated into philosophical terms. (#MJ1778—$1.95)

☐ **THE AGE OF ANALYSIS: 20th Century Philosophers edited by Morton White.** Basic writings of Peirce, Whitehead, James, Croce, Santayana, Dewey, Sartre, and others, covering such problems as logic, philosophical and linguistic analysis, existentialism, phenomenology, and time.
(#ME1847—$1.75)